12 Unforgettable Men of the Gospels

REFLECTIONS AND PORTRAITS OF THE APOSTLES

Melanie Rigney

Twenty-Third Publications
977 Hartford Turnpike Unit A
Waterford, CT 06385
(860) 437-3012 or (800) 321-0411
twentythirdpublications.com

ISBN: 978-1-62785-865-6
Printed in the U.S.A.

CONTENTS

INTRODUCTION

You see them on stained glass in your parish or a retreat center or a museum. You hear their names in gospel readings and on their feast days.

Jesus called the Twelve as apostles during his earthly ministry, selecting them to go out and preach the good news to the world. The larger group of disciples (think of them as students or followers) included many more, including women. But beyond Peter, who is typically shown as an old man with a gray beard, and John, who is typically shown as a young man with long hair, it can be difficult for all of us to remember the names of the Twelve, let alone their relationships and who did and said what, went where after Pentecost, and died how.

In this book, my goal is to get the men Jesus chose off the stained glass and into your heart and soul—even Judas, who has some cautionary lessons to teach us. They were people, just as we are. Most of them likely were not well traveled or well educated. They had fears and prejudices and tempers just like us. And Jesus took it all, the good and the bad in each of them, and offered a path none of them could have imagined. He does the same with us.

Each chapter shares what we know about the man, through Scripture or Sacred Tradition. You'll find Old Testament Scripture that the apostle may have known and that is related to his particular gift or challenge. There's also a story about being the apostle today (or learning from his faith to overcome a deficit). Three questions to discuss or ponder appropriate for individual or group use are included, along with a prayer and some looks at paintings or drawings of the man. One image for each is shown. You'll also find the title and artist for all the images along with a web link and a description in case you'd rather not search for the image. Lastly, you'll find a short biography on someone beatified or canonized in this century who lived the apostle's gift or challenge and "A Deeper Dive" featuring thoughts from a pope or minister about the apostle.

My prayer is that you find an apostle, well known or obscure, who resonates with you. Jesus chose these men, each for a purpose. Maybe for one of them, a purpose was to pray with you, today, in the twenty-first century. Let's find out.

Here's a quick list in the order brought forth in Matthew 10:2–4. It's the same order we'll study them here:

PETER (also known as Simon) **AND HIS BROTHER ANDREW**, both fishermen who grew up in Bethsaida on Lake Genesareth. Their father was Jonah. Earlier, Andrew was a follower of John the Baptist.

JAMES AND JOHN, Galilean fishermen who knew Peter and Andrew. Their father was Zebedee; some believe their mother was Mary Salome, a sister or half-sister of the Blessed Virgin. James is sometimes called James the Great or Greater to distinguish him from James son of Alphaeus. John is sometimes called the beloved disciple or John the Evangelist.

PHILIP, also from Bethsaida, who was among those near John the Baptist when he called Jesus the Lamb of God; friend of Bartholomew.

BARTHOLOMEW, who is the same man as Nathanael (Bartholomew appears to be his family name, Bar-Tolmai, son of Tolmai); friend of Philip.

THOMAS, about whose pre-Jesus life we know almost nothing other than that he likely was from Galilee and likely was a twin.

MATTHEW, a Galilean and tax collector, sometimes called Levi. His father was named Alphaeus, which was not an uncommon name; whether he and the apostle James son of Alphaeus were brothers is unclear.

JAMES SON OF ALPHAEUS. He is often called James the Less or Little James to distinguish him from James son of Zebedee. He likely was a relative of Jesus and may have been the son of Mary, the wife of Clopas, who was at the foot of the cross. Some believe she was the Blessed Virgin's sister, half-sister, or sister-in-law. One early writer identified James as the brother of Jude Thaddeus and Simon the Zealot, though the gospels do not indicate this.

JUDE OR JUDE THADDAEUS: He came to Jerusalem in John the Baptist's days and was baptized by him. The name Lebbaeus is also associated with him. Either his brother or father was named James. One early writer identified him as the brother of James son of Alphaeus and Simon the Zealot, though the gospels do not mention this.

SIMON THE ZEALOT OR CANANAEAN: One early writer identified him as the brother of James son of Alphaeus and Jude Thaddaeus, though the gospels do not say this.

JUDAS ISCARIOT: He likely was from the southern Judea town of Kerioth-hezron, near what is now the border between Israel and Egypt.

Peter

THE ONE WHO SPOKE OUT

DEATH: Around 66 AD in Rome

FEAST DAY: June 29 (with St. Paul)

SCRIPTURE: [Jesus] said to them, "But who do you say that I am?" Simon Peter answered, "You are the Messiah, the Son of the living God." ■ **MATTHEW 16:15–16**

Who Was Peter?

Not surprisingly, Peter appears more often in the New Testament than any of the other eleven apostles. He has a lot to say, learn—and teach us.

This apostle begins life as Simon but becomes Peter, the rock, during Jesus' earthly ministry. When this happens varies by gospel writer (Matthew 16:17–18; John 1:42). For purposes of this study, the apostle will be called Peter except when Scripture calls him Simon.

Peter is part of Jesus' inner circle, along with James and John, the sons of Zebedee and his fishing business partners (Luke 5:10). They are alone with Jesus at the healing of Jairus's daughter (Luke 8:41–56; Mark 5:22–24, 35–43), the Transfiguration (Mark 9:2–8; Luke 9:28–36; Matthew 17:1–8), and the agony in the garden (Mark 14:33–42; Matthew 26:37–46). These three, joined by Peter's brother Andrew, are present when Jesus heals Peter's mother-in-law (Mark 1:29–31). The four are with Jesus when he speaks of persecutions and violence to come outside the temple following his triumphal entry into Jerusalem (Mark 13:3–8).

Peter's words at the Last Supper and the hours thereafter will be discussed later in this chapter.

We don't know where Peter or most of the apostles were as Jesus was crucified; they may have been among the acquaintances Luke 23:49 says were standing at a distance. In Luke 24:12 and John 20:1–7, Peter enters the tomb on Easter Monday and finds the linen cloths but not Jesus. Luke describes him as "amazed at what had happened."

Peter is present with the others for the coming of the Holy Spirit (Acts 1:13). Then, his trust and passion are on full display throughout Acts, preaching and healing, unafraid of the earthly consequences despite persecution and imprisonment.

He also wrote letters to the Christian communities in Asia Minor (1 Peter and 2 Peter). The opening of each letter identifies the author as an apostle; some scholars believe that while the letters reflect Peter's preaching and words, they were recorded by someone else. The first letter seeks to encourage the communities to embrace Jesus' message despite persecution; the second focuses on a vision of the second coming and encourages the audience to be faithful.

Peter was the early Church's leader in Jerusalem and later evangelized far and wide in the East, occasionally returning to Jerusalem. His later years were spent in Rome, where he was martyred in about 66 AD. Tradition holds that he was crucified with his head down because he felt he was unworthy of dying in the same manner as Jesus.

Tradition says that the Basilica of St. Peter in the Vatican was built over his tomb. An exhaustive examination in the 1960s found bones in a marble-lined repository beneath the basilica to be those of a man about five feet six inches in his sixties who had died in the first century. Pope Paul VI in 1968 said they are most likely Peter's relics.

PETER THE MAN

Today, we'd call Peter a man without filters. He speaks his mind freely, even to (or, perhaps, especially to) Jesus. He is impetuous, arrogant, and obtuse, asking the questions and making the brash pronouncements none of the others would. By turns, Jesus listens, praises, and rebukes him, grooming him for his eventual role as the leader not only of the apostles but of the Church on earth after the Ascension.

Consider:

- After Jesus talks about the difficulty of a rich person entering heaven, Peter asks what the Twelve will get since they've given up everything for him (Mark 10:28; Matthew 19:27; Luke 18:28).
- As Jesus walks toward the apostles' storm-battered boat, Peter says that if it's truly the Lord walking on the water, he should call Peter to come. Jesus does, and lo and behold, Peter can walk on water too—until he realizes he's walking on water and begins to sink (Matthew 14:22–31).
- Peter asks if the disciples really must forgive as many as seven times. Jesus says not seven times, but seventy-seven, implying an infinite number (Matthew 18:21–22).

Jesus knew what was inside Peter's heart and chastised him only occasionally. But the Lord could be strong in those corrections:

Old Testament Scripture on **Speaking Out**

DEUTERONOMY 31:6

Moses shares with Israel shortly before his death that God has told him: "Be strong and bold...it is the Lord your God who goes with you; he will not fail you or forsake you."

PROVERBS 28:1

Solomon notes that "the wicked flee when no one pursues, but the righteous are as bold as a lion."

EXODUS 4:12

When Moses says he isn't well spoken and thus should not be the one to lead the people, the Lord tells him, "Now go, and I will be with your mouth and teach you what you are to speak."

- Jesus asks, "Are you also still without understanding?" after Peter requests an explanation of the parable on defilement (Matthew 15:16).
- After Jesus has begun to tell the disciples what will happen in Jerusalem, including his death and resurrection, Peter takes him aside and says this must never happen. Jesus rebukes him in the strongest of terms: "Get behind me, Satan! You are a hindrance to me, for you are setting your mind not on divine things but on human things" (Matthew 16:21–23; Mark 8:31–33).

Yet, Peter also can be almost achingly perceptive.

- Early on, Peter and Jesus are on Peter's boat. It's been a bad night; Peter has netted no fish. Jesus tells him to let down the nets one more time. Peter seems a little less than convinced but does so, and the nets fill to overflowing. Peter doesn't dance for joy or even immediately thank Jesus. He recognizes the import of the moment and his own inadequacy, falls at Jesus' knees, and says, "Go away from me, Lord, for I am a sinful man!" (Luke 5:8). Jesus tells him not to fear; going forward, Peter will be catching people.
- Others are quick to respond when Jesus asks who the people say he is, with answers that strain our credulity today: John the Baptist (who has already been beheaded at this point)? Elijah? Jeremiah? Another long-dead prophet? Only Peter answers when Jesus asks who the disciples say he is: "the Messiah, the Son of the living God" (Matthew 16:16; also Mark 8:29 and Luke 9:20).

Peter's filters are most painfully lacking at the Last Supper and in the following hours. First, he doesn't want Jesus to wash his feet;

Jesus says Peter will have "no share" with him in that case. Peter then overcompensates, saying Jesus should also wash his hands and head (John 13:6–9). A bit later, Jesus says one of the Twelve will betray him and Peter will deny him three times in the next few hours. Peter vigorously disputes this according to all four gospels, then proceeds to do just that. Matthew, Mark, and Luke all report Peter weeping upon realizing what he had done.

But he still doesn't understand, not exactly, not even after he's seen the risen Christ twice (when Jesus appears to them all except Thomas, and then again to all the eleven a week later). The third time, Peter has organized a fishing expedition with six other apostles (John 21:1–14). They've been out all night and caught nothing. They don't recognize Jesus when he calls to them from the beach and tells them to cast out once more, reminiscent of Jesus' original call to Peter, Andrew, and the sons of Zebedee in Luke 5. Peter is so excited he dons his outer garment and jumps into the sea. Jesus has already started a fire with fish on it.

When breakfast is finished, Jesus gives Peter his commission. Three times, he asks a variant of whether Peter loves him. Three times, Peter says yes, wondering why Jesus doubts him. Each time, Jesus asks him to care for his sheep. Then Jesus foretells Peter's own martyrdom and again says, "Follow me." And Peter does.

Yes, Peter lacked filters. But he came as he was to Jesus, and his faith and trust have inspired generations. He is us in our struggles and lack of understanding. We hope to be him in his confidence and boldness and contrition. He shows us that speaking out gets us closer to Jesus than closeting our questions and fears.

BEING PETER TODAY

While we may roll our eyes about Peter being so excited that he wanted to build tents to make the Transfiguration last or shake our heads and sigh about those three denials, we've all spoken too quickly and regretted it. We're human.

But as time went on—was the "feed my sheep" direction a conversion moment for him?—he matured. He listened. He led. And yes, he fed Jesus' sheep and lambs.

Priests and deacons sometimes speak too quickly too. Life circumstances—a crisis in the parish school, a broken HVAC system in the parish center, a parishioner who wants to go point by point over why the last homily stunk—can make them less than thoughtful or compassionate if we're the next person who encounters them. Like Peter and like us, they're human.

Here are some of the holy moments with priests that I remember when I am tempted to complain about a boring homily or whine about a brusque dismissal in the confessional or after Mass:

- A pre-dawn Advent novena Mass celebrated (signed and spoken) by the second deaf person to be ordained a priest in the United States. When he looked heavenward during the liturgy, you knew from the expression and glow on his face that he was in conversation with the Lord, not merely reciting words he'd said thousands of times before or mailing it in because he'd had to get up so early. By his example and his pithy homily on doing God's will, he challenged us not to mail it in either.
- A homily by a priest whose words didn't typically speak to me. He shared that he went through several dark years of drinking and near homelessness in early adulthood. A movie prompted him to crawl out of despair, change his name, convert to Catholicism, and eventually become a priest.

- A priest who faced angry parishioners in Africa shortly after being ordained. He had heard the deathbed confession of a woman who practiced sorcery and, believing the confession to be true, baptized her. She asked to be buried in the parish cemetery and he agreed. Parishioners who believed they had been injured by her were outraged and went to the bishop. The priest stood by his belief, and the bishop supported him.
- The early Mass the morning after I'd had a stormy counseling session with my pastor. The early Mass was my usual routine, and I knew he'd be presiding. I thought about not going but realized if I didn't go then, regardless of what he might do or say, I'd never go again. During the sign of peace, he came off the altar to shake my hand.

PONDERING OUTSPOKENNESS

- Read aloud John 21:17, the third time Jesus asks Peter if he loves him. Where is Jesus asking you to feed his sheep in a way that is a bit out of your comfort zone? Maybe you feel a nudge to join a new-to-you ministry or to reach out to someone you haven't seen in a while.
- Peter contradicted Jesus at the Last Supper, saying he would never betray the Lord—and then did within a few hours. Think about a time that you judged someone's words or behavior, only to find yourself reacting the same way in a similar situation. Maybe it involved the way you raise your children or care for your grandchildren, or your reaction to a difficult circumstance at work. Consider taking this to confession and possibly apologizing to the other person.

- Speaking out about what you believe as a Catholic Christian can get you ridiculed and isolated. This week, put those fears aside and speak truth in a loving way to someone who needs it.

PETER IN IMAGES

Spanish painter Jusepe de Ribera (1591–1652), in *The Tears of Saint Peter,*[1] shows Peter at his very lowest, after he has denied Jesus three times—and has realized that that is just what Jesus had said he would do. There are tears on his face, which is red with emotion. He kneels and looks toward heaven, which he knows is the only place he can find forgiveness and rest.

What sin are you holding tight because you are sure it can't be forgiven? It cannot be worse than having denied Jesus at his greatest hour of human need. Resolve to go to confession or schedule a pastoral counseling session.

In *The Apostle Saint Peter,*[2] Flemish painter Peter Paul Rubens (1577–1640) shows Peter as pope, holding the keys to heaven, which Jesus promised him in Matthew 16:19. The apostle's posture is confident; his eyes look above, but with a different emotion than in the Ribera painting—humility or dependence, perhaps?

Consider journaling about a time you felt in communion with the Holy Trinity because you stopped trying to solve a problem or hurt on your own and prayed for help.

PRAYER

St. Peter, your stumbles inspire me as much as your faith. Whenever you fell, your trust in Jesus' mercy and forgiveness brought you back to him. Please pray that I may learn from your example. Amen.

Another Who Spoke Out

ST. TITUS BRANDSMA *(1881–1942)*

CANONIZED MAY 15, 2022 ✠ FEAST DAY: JULY 27

Like Peter, this Dutch priest spoke out and paid the ultimate price.

Anno Brandsma's parents were dairy farmers and devout Catholics, living in a Calvinist area of the Netherlands. They passed their faith onto their six children, and five of them entered religious life.

Anno was drawn to the Carmelites' mysticism and was ordained as a priest in his mid-twenties, taking the name Titus to honor his father. But he also had a calling as an educator, journalist, and writer and was not cloistered. He was a founder of a Catholic university in the Netherlands, where he also lectured and taught, and served as the school's president in 1932–33.

For Titus, 1935 was a seminal year. Adolf Hitler and the Nazi Party had gained total power in Germany the year before. Titus saw the dangers of the movement and its devaluing of people, calling Nazism a "black lie" and "pagan." He went on a speaking tour in the United States and Canada, and back at home became the spiritual director of the Union of Catholic Journalists. He began to catch the attention of Nazi leaders in Germany for his outspokenness and his work as the board chair for the Dutch Catholic high schools organization.

The Nazis invaded the Netherlands in May 1940 and had control of the country in less than a week. Eventually, the occupiers made it mandatory for newspapers to print news releases and accept advertising from their party. The Dutch bishops' conference developed a letter requiring Catholic newspapers to resist the law and sent Titus to deliver it. He was arrested in January 1942 after having visited fourteen editors.

Titus was held at a series of prisons before being sent to the Dachau concentration camp that June. Other prisoners said he was kicked and beaten to the point his teeth were loosened. He provided a daily blessing to other inmates and heard confessions in violation of a ban on priestly ministry. He died after less than a month at Dachau from a carbolic acid injection that was part of a medical experimentation program. He told the nurse who administered the injection he would pray for her. She later said she returned to Catholicism because of Titus.

A DEEPER DIVE

From the naïve enthusiasm of initial acceptance, passing though the sorrowful experience of denial and the weeping of conversion, Peter succeeded in entrusting himself to that Jesus who adapted himself to his poor capacity of love. And in this way he shows us the way, notwithstanding all of our weakness. We know that Jesus adapts himself to this weakness of ours.

■ **POPE BENEDICT XVI,** *General Audience, May 24, 2006*[3]

Andrew

THE ONE WHO CONNECTED

DEATH: Around 60 AD in Greece

FEAST DAY: November 30

SCRIPTURE: [Andrew] first found his brother Simon and said to him, "We have found the Messiah" (which is translated Anointed). ■ **JOHN 1:41**

Who Was Andrew?

Andrew is identified as one of the Twelve in each of the synoptic gospels (Mark 3:18; Matthew 10:2; Luke 6:14). Matthew (4:18–20) and Mark (1:16–18) also describe Jesus calling Andrew and his brother Peter as the first disciples. Who was older is uncertain.

The Gospel of John's version of Andrew's first encounter with Jesus is a bit different. In John 1:35–42, Andrew and another, unnamed, disciple of John the Baptist are there when Jesus walks by, and the baptizer exclaims, "Look, here is the Lamb of God!" The two follow immediately and stay with Jesus. Then Andrew finds Peter, says, "We have found the Messiah," and brings him to Jesus. For this reason, the Orthodox Church refers to Andrew as the *Protokletos (Protoclete)*, meaning the first called.

Andrew is also mentioned as being at Peter's home when Jesus heals Peter's mother-in-law and then in the evening heals a host of people (Mark 1:29–34).

We see Andrew on three more occasions before the crucifixion.

- After Jesus denounces the scribes and goes to the Mount of Olives opposite the temple, Andrew, Peter, James, and John approach him privately and ask when the temple will be destroyed and what the signs will be (Mark 13:3–4).
- When Jesus asks where the disciples can buy bread at the feeding of the five thousand, Andrew is one of two who respond. He says, "There is a boy here who has five barley loaves and two fish. But what are they among so many people?" (John 6:9).
- After the triumphal entry into Jerusalem, some Greeks who have come to worship at Passover approach Philip about seeing Jesus. Philip tells Andrew, and the two of them go to speak with Jesus. He tells them the hour has come for him to be glorified (John 12:20–23).

Andrew was at the Last Supper with the others, of course. We don't know where he or most of the apostles were as Jesus was crucified; they may have been among the acquaintances Luke 23:49 says were standing at a distance.

Andrew also appears with the others in Acts 1:13 at the coming of the Holy Spirit.

Scholars believe that Andrew's evangelization primarily took place in what is now Ukraine and southern Russia, Asia Minor, and Greece, where he was martyred. Tradition holds that he was crucified on a cross in the form of the letter X and that he was not nailed to the cross but tied with ropes so his suffering would be prolonged. He died after two days.

Tradition is that Andrew's relics were moved to Istanbul in 357, then eventually to St. Peter's Basilica in Rome.

ANDREW THE MAN

Andrew's name means "manly" in Greek, while his brother Simon's name ("to hear") is Hebrew. That tells us a bit about the influence Greek language and culture had on Galilee at the time. It was not unusual for people of that time to speak multiple languages, which helps explain why the Gentile Greeks approach Philip in Jerusalem to meet Jesus. Philip very well may have spoken Greek, too, but he doesn't take the Greeks to Jesus directly. He goes to Andrew because connecting people, especially with Jesus, is what Andrew does.

We know that Andrew, like his brother, was a fisherman. Unlike with the sons of Zebedee, we see no evidence in the gospels of any rivalry between Andrew and his brother or anyone else. There's no evidence of him feeling slighted when he doesn't get the alone time with Jesus that Peter, James, and John do. He doesn't struggle as much with what Jesus means or what that may mean to Andrew personally. The only time this is even hinted at is when Andrew joins the three at the Mount of Olives to ask about Jesus' foretelling of the temple's destruction, both literally and metaphorically.

Andrew's finest moment comes at the feeding of the five thousand. Jesus asks the disciples where they can buy food for the people. John 6:6 tells us it was a test; Jesus already knew what he was going to do. In rabbinical style, Philip doesn't answer Jesus' question. He instead says that even if they had six months' wages, it wouldn't be enough to buy even a bit for the entire crowd.

Old Testament Scripture on **Connection**

WISDOM 7:14
Solomon extols the importance of wisdom and says, "those who get it obtain friendship with God."

SIRACH 6:16
Ben Sira provides guidance on how to find true friends and says, "Faithful friends are life-saving medicine; and those who fear the Lord will find them."

MICAH 6:8
The prophet shares God's requirements for the people, not burnt offerings "but to do justice, and to love kindness, and to walk humbly with your God."

Andrew takes Jesus literally. Where to get food? Well, there's a kid who has five barley loaves and two fish. He adds, "But what are they among so many people?" (John 6:9). Then he waits and trusts. He doesn't ask Jesus what the Twelve should do. He doesn't despair. He doesn't demand to know what Jesus is going to do about this situation.

The apostle appears to have had people's respect and trust, as the examples above show. Further, he is mentioned in the Muratorian fragment, an eighty-five-line Latin manuscript that may date from the second century. Some consider it the oldest known list of many of what became the books of the New Testament. Within this document is information about the writing of John's gospel. John asks the bishops and disciples who want him to write the account to join him in three days' fasting for discernment. The very first night, according to the fragment, "it was revealed to Andrew, [one] of the apostles, that John should write down all things in his own name while all of them should review it."[4]

Indeed, a few scholars have posited that Andrew, not John, may be the unnamed "beloved disciple" in John's gospel. That, however, is not Roman Catholic Church teaching.

Regardless, Andrew continues to bring people together in modern times. In 1964, Pope Paul VI traveled to Jerusalem, the first pope to do so. While there, he met with Ecumenical Patriarch of Constantinople Athenagoras. It was the first meeting of the leaders of the two flocks in a thousand years. In a sign of friendship, Pope Paul VI brought the ecumenical patriarch the skull of Andrew. That relic and Andrew's cross are now housed at the Greek Orthodox Cathedral of St. Andrew in Patras, Greece.[5]

BEING ANDREW TODAY

My former colleague Gerry never met a stranger. You know people like him, cracking jokes and playing the clown to make everyone feel at ease. People, I think, like Andrew.

I met Gerry after I'd been with the federal government about six months. I had pretty much kept my head down those first six months and worked on learning the new job and the new city, not interacting casually with my coworkers. Then an opportunity came up to volunteer for the government's annual charity drive. There was an off-site training meeting one hot day in August, and Gerry was the only one there who looked familiar. When the meeting was over, he rushed over, said he recognized me, and asked if we could walk the ten blocks back to the office together. I thought it was kind of crazy not to take public transit given the heat, but said, "All right."

I didn't have to say much as we walked; he was pointing out the sights and guessing where the tourist were from. He made me laugh, and I hadn't laughed in quite a while.

The next thing I knew, Gerry was introducing me to other coworkers. He'd get a group together for lunch once a week or so, whoever was available. He didn't mind that I always brought a sandwich from home; the days I could make it, lunch would be outside. Gerry had one rule: we couldn't talk about work or politics. He said we should talk about important things, like our families and sports. Baseball was his big love, and he would organize outings to the ballpark toward the end of the season when the Washington Nationals were out of the playoff picture so seats were cheap.

If there was a charity event that needed a treasurer (we did work for the U.S. Department of the Treasury, after all), Gerry was there. He'd often recruit a bunch of us to help with checking in participants or distributing snacks or water bottles. He was the commissioner for Catholic Youth Organization basketball in his area, a responsibility he took very seriously, and also did some pro bono coaching for the kids.

Once I asked him why he did all this, thinking that maybe it was to find a girlfriend or because he was lonely. He gave me a pitying look and said, "I just like to get people together. If we can help people, that's even better."

And help people he did. He and I both stayed involved in the big federal charity drive, and one year he grew out his bushy gray hair for six months, then people donated to be among those who "sheared" him. When my first solo book was published, he arranged for me to speak to the women at his parish. Sometimes, his help went a little too far. At one point, he was making payments on two cars besides his own because he had cosigned notes and then the people disappeared with the vehicles.

I don't see Gerry as much as I should now that we're both retired and his place isn't accessible by public transit. But I think of him every time I meet someone who looks a little lost and out of his or her depth. Like Andrew, Gerry taught me that getting people together—and helping them—is what the Lord desires.

PONDERING CONNECTION

- Read aloud John 1:35–42. Consider how excited Andrew was to share Jesus with his brother. What Scripture or spiritual practice most speaks to your soul, and how can you share that passion with someone whose faith is lukewarm?

- Andrew directly answered Jesus' question about where bread (and a couple of fish!) could be found, then waited for Jesus to show his followers what would happen next. Think about a question Jesus is asking you, and you are choosing not to answer, perhaps because you don't want to take on the changes or actions he desires.
- Andrew appears to have been satisfied with his role among the Twelve—and well he should have been, traveling with Jesus, dining with him, listening to his wisdom. Jesus is present in our lives, too, always. Where are you taking that gift for granted?

ANDREW IN IMAGES

In *The Calling of Saints Peter and Andrew*, Italian painter Caravaggio (1571–1610) places the least emphasis on Andrew, who is the man with red hair. Jesus is on the right; Peter is on the left.[6]

In the painting, Andrew points his index finger at his brother, almost as if he's saying to Jesus, "You need this one!" Why do you think the painter showed Andrew pointing at Peter rather than Jesus?

In *St. Andrew,*[7] Flemish painter Artus Wolffort (1581–1641) shows us an aged apostle poring over a book. He seems to be intent... or perhaps asleep. Quill and ink are in the foreground; the scene appears to be within a cave. The legend under his name translates to "and in Jesus Christ, his only Son our Lord."

Do you ever lose track of time and place when you are at adoration or deep in prayer? Consider journaling about the experience so you can remember it during times of spiritual drought and trust that the dryness will end.

PRAYER

St. Andrew, please help me to set aside my jealousy and envy of those who are closer to my pastor and other leaders than I am. Help me to follow your example of trusting Jesus and introducing others to him. Amen.

Another Who Connected
ST. CARLO ACUTIS *(1991–2006)*

CANONIZED SEPTEMBER 7, 2025 — FEAST DAY: OCTOBER 12

Some call him the first millennial saint; others, the patron saint of the internet. One of his quotes says it best—"To always be close to Jesus, that's my plan"[8]—and during his short life, the teenager brought a lot of people along with him.

Carlo was born in London to parents from wealthy Italian families. The family moved back to Italy when he was an infant. His devotion to the Rosary began when he was very young, and he was a frequent daily communicant. His zeal inspired a reversion to an active faith life for his mother and the conversion of a household worker and the worker's friend and mother.

Carlo used his programming skills to connect people with Jesus. He created an award-winning website to promote volunteerism at his parish and another showing all reported eucharistic miracles in the world.[9] It was launched on October 4, 2006, shortly after Carlo had fallen ill with what would soon be determined was leukemia. He died on October 12 that same year.

A DEEPER DIVE

The apostle Andrew, therefore, teaches us to follow Jesus with promptness (cf. Mt 4:20; Mk 1:18), to speak enthusiastically about him to those we meet, and especially, to cultivate a relationship of true familiarity with him, acutely aware that in him alone can we find the ultimate meaning of our life and death.

■ **POPE BENEDICT XVI**, *General Audience, June 14, 2006*[10]

James

THE AMBITIOUS ONE

DEATH: 44 AD in Jerusalem

FEAST DAY: July 25

SCRIPTURE: And (James and John) said to him, "Appoint us to sit, one at your right hand and one at your left, in your glory."
■ **MARK 10:37**

Who Was James?

James is identified as one of the Twelve in each of the synoptic gospels (Mark 3:17; Matthew 10:2; Luke 6:14). Mark 1:19–20 and Matthew 4:21–22 say that Jesus called James and his brother John while they were with their father, Zebedee, mending their fishing nets, and that the brothers immediately left and followed. Luke 5:1–11 shows the sons of Zebedee being among those present for Peter's big catch, then bringing their boats to shore and following.

The apostle likely is known as James the Great or Greater because he was taller or older or began following Jesus before James son of Alphaeus. There is general agreement that this James was not the author of the Letter of James in the New Testament.

James held a special place among the Twelve along with John and Peter. They are alone with Jesus at the healing of Jairus's daughter (Luke 8:41–42, 48–56; Mark 5:22–24, 35–43), the Transfiguration (Mark 9:2–8; Luke 9:28–36; Matthew 17:1–8), and the agony in the garden (Mark 14:33–42; Matthew 26:37–46). Luke 22:45 says the disciples were sleeping "because of grief" while Jesus prayed after the Last Supper but does not identify them.

These three, joined by Peter's brother, Andrew, are present when Jesus heals Peter's mother-in-law (Mark 1:29–31). According to Mark 13:3–8, these four are with Jesus when he speaks of persecutions and violence to come.

Scripture provides some clues about the personalities of James and John. Mark 3:17 groups the pair and adds, parenthetically, "(to whom he gave the name Boanerges, that is, Sons of Thunder"). And, as the followers pass through a Samaritan village, Jesus rebukes the brothers when they ask if the two of them should "command fire to come down from heaven and consume" the villagers (Luke 9:54–55) for not receiving them. Further, we see Jesus reproach them when they (Mark 10:35–44) or their mother (Matthew 20:20–27) ask that James and John be seated at his right and left in glory.

Later, James is among the seven disciples who don't initially recognize the risen Lord when they go fishing (John 21:2).

He appears with the others in Acts 1:13 at the coming of the Holy Spirit, and his martyrdom by sword ordered by King Herod is briefly chronicled at Acts 12:2. That makes him the only one of the eleven whose death is recorded in the New Testament.

Some believe that James evangelized in Spain before returning to Jerusalem and that his remains were sent to Compostela in northwest Spain. This seems unlikely since in Romans 15:20, Paul indicates he plans to visit Spain shortly after, saying he will take the gospel "not where Christ has already been named, so that I do not build on someone else's foundation." Regardless, the legend inspires about half a million people annually to make pilgrimages on one of several routes on foot, bicycle, or horseback to visit the Santiago de Compostela Cathedral, built over what are said to be James's relics.

JAMES THE MAN

Should it really surprise us that Jesus could choose as one of the Twelve an overachieving child whose parents were prominent members of their community?

Zebedee, Salome, and their family likely lived in or near Bethsaida, possibly in Capernaum. Zebedee's fishing business must have been doing well; we know he had hired hands in addition to James and John. As for Salome, she may have been the sister or half-sister of the Blessed Virgin Mary.

Was it expected that James in particular as the older son (assuming James and John were Zebedee and Salome's only children) would eventually take over the family fishing enterprise? Possibly. Under rabbinic law, the oldest son receives a double portion of the estate upon the father's death. So, if there were two sons, the estate would be divided into three parts, with the older receiving two parts.

We don't know why Jesus nicknamed the brothers "Sons of Thunder." But based on what we see about them offering to call down lightning for Jesus (the utter audacity of it!) and their (and their mother's) request for places of honor, it's easy to see a sense of entitlement and privilege. James may have been used to giving the workers orders and making day-to-day decisions if Zebedee was away and may have assumed he would have a similar role in Jesus' ministry.

Given all this, it likely chafed James's ego a bit—maybe more than a bit—that according to John (1:42), Jesus renamed Simon "Peter," or "Cephas," the first time they met. James and Peter knew

Old Testament Scripture on **Ambition**

PROVERBS 3:5–6
Solomon urges the people to "Trust in the Lord with all your heart" and "acknowledge him" rather than relying on themselves.

PSALM 37:3–4
David says the desires of one's heart and security will result from trusting and taking delight in the Lord.

ISAIAH 55:8–9
Through the prophet, God reminds the people that the Almighty's thoughts and ways are higher than theirs.

each other before Jesus began calling the apostles, and one wonders how their relationship was affected by Simon's designation as the one on whom the Church would be built.

There's also a certain tone deafness in Mark 10:35–37, when James and John ask to sit at Jesus' right and left in his kingdom. Jesus has just foretold his death and resurrection for the third time, but the brothers see this as the time to push themselves forward. The timing is the same when their mother makes the request in Matthew 20:20–21 and the sons affirm they are ready to drink from the cup. Small wonder the other apostles become angry!

And yet—Jesus recognizes James's potential. He makes James part of the inner circle. He tells James and John that they will indeed drink from his cup, and they don't run away or back away, though they likely did not fully comprehend what that could entail.

I'd like to think that Jesus' words immediately after the sons of Zebedee's audacious request spoke to James's heart and soul and began the conversion of his ambition for personal recognition and success into a zeal to serve Jesus. The words in Matthew's and Mark's gospels are similar, but I like Mark's just a bit better:

> "You know that among the gentiles those whom they recognize as their rules lord it over them, and their great ones are tyrants over them. But it is not so among you; instead, whoever wishes to become great among you must be your servant, and whoever wishes to be first among you must be slave of all. For the Son of Man came not to be served but to serve and to give his life a ransom for many." ■ *Mark 10:42–45*

James doesn't appear again in the gospels until his failure, along with that of Peter and John, to stay awake as Jesus prays after the Last Supper. We don't know where James or most of the apostles were as

Jesus was crucified; they may have been among the acquaintances Luke 23:49 says were standing at a distance. Perhaps James thought then about his and his brother's brash promise that they were ready to drink the same cup as Jesus. Jesus' words may have come back as cold, hard reality now, not a lovely metaphor. Would James be up for the challenge?

James was among the six apostles who joined Peter on a fishing expedition but caught nothing until just after daybreak, when the risen Lord, unrecognized to them, calls from the shore to put out their nets once more (John 21:1–8). Perhaps that intimate, personal moment and the coming of the Holy Spirit sealed James's conversion.

The once personally ambitious apostle became the first to be martyred for the faith. One early work says the man who brought James to his execution was so moved by the way the apostle conducted himself that he confessed he, too, was a Christian; as they were being taken away, he asked James for forgiveness. James said, "Peace be with you," and kissed him before they were both executed.[11]

BEING JAMES TODAY

People sometimes ask me why my ex-husband and I never had children. I generally say that I'm the oldest daughter of an oldest daughter of an oldest daughter of an oldest daughter (true!) and all that hyper-responsibleness had to end. It always gets a laugh.

I'm not entirely joking.

Unlike James, I was the oldest of four in a lower-middle-class family. My dad worked construction and night security jobs until he got on as a postal service clerk, and Mom stayed at home until I was in high school. Unlike my friends' parents, they never seemed particularly surprised or proud of me when I got a debate trophy or newspaper award. They never put pressure on me to get good grades or earn honors. I put enough pressure on myself for that, from kindergarten posture and color queen to professional positions decades later.

I spent years striving to get the next good report card, the next good job, and so on. I wasn't the sort who was envious of those who excelled beyond me; I would just beat myself up for not having finished on top, trying to figure out on my own where I had failed so I could do better the next time.

Yes, I've been through therapy, and it helped. But some of this is just hard wired. So, when I read the gospel references about James the Great, my heart breaks just a bit for him because I see myself as he and his brother try to get a leg up in a competition that never existed.

As with James, what helped me the most was slowly realizing that Jesus' love isn't based on how much money I've made, how many books I've written, or how much engagement I get on social media. Jesus loves me. If I had become a teenage ax murderer, he would have loved me just as much. But if I wish to please him and honor him as he desires, that means not walking away from difficult conversations about Catholic beliefs. It means being willing to accept that some people I considered friends keep their distance these days because my views on polarizing issues aren't the same as theirs, and I won't and can't stay silent.

I highly doubt Jesus intends most of us to be physical martyrs for our faith. But should that situation come to be, we are asked to accept it with the grace that James, who once was focused on moving ahead the way the world desires, did.

PONDERING AMBITION

- What expectations did your family of origin place on you? Maybe it was to go to a particular college or get a particular kind of job or marry a particular type of person. Were you able to discern God's desire and place that above human expectations? Either way, how did things work out?

- Ambition can happen in our faith lives too. Have you gossiped about how much better your voice or that of friend or family member is than the cantor at last Sunday's Mass? Or maybe it was about the way someone proclaimed a reading or ran a ministry meeting. Take it to Jesus through the Sacrament of Penance and Reconciliation.
- Where is your own need for recognition tainting your prayer life? Are you always about ask-ask-ask and me-me-me when you pray instead of listening to the Lord? Monitor yourself today. Consider changing your position or posture when you start to make it all about you.

JAMES IN IMAGES

The model used by Spanish painter Jusepe de Ribera (1591–1652) for his work *St. James the Greater*[12] is young, almost boyish. He is nearly dwarfed by his red robe. The face appears gentle and at peace, not what we might expect of a Son of Thunder during Jesus' earthly ministry.

After you've spent some time with this image, look at your face in the mirror. Are there worry lines? A frown? Spend five to ten minutes in silence or saying a prayer that resonates with you, then look again. Is there more peace in your gaze?

Another Spanish painter of the same era, Bartolomé Esteban Murillo (1617–82), in *The Apostle Saint James*, shows us an older James.[13] He is depicted with a scallop shell, which serves as the symbol to help those making pilgrimages to Compostela. Murillo shows us a strong, forceful James: his eyebrows are raised in a powerful way, as if someone has just questioned him about his faith.

Is there something you could adopt as your sign of faith so others know you are Catholic, just as the Compostela pilgrims look for the scallop shell? Maybe it's a crucifix necklace or bracelet or other piece of jewelry you could always wear. Or maybe it's an image or prayer that is your background in social media. Are there other visible signs you can share?

PRAYER

St. James, you truly converted when you stopped being ambitious for yourself and put that force and energy into evangelizing and serving Christ. I ask that you intercede for me, that I put my worldly goals in the background and focus on service. Amen.

Another Ambitious One

ST. MATTHEW AYARIGA

(died February 2015)

CANONIZED OCTOBER 20, 2024, AS A MEMBER OF THE 21 COPTIC MARTYRS OF LIBYA ❧ FEAST DAY: FEBRUARY 15

Of this much, we are sure: Matthew was born in Ghana or possibly Chad, probably in the 1980s or 1990s.

He left his home looking for a better life, and that's the kind of ambition the world generally approves of: people looking for ways to feed themselves and their families or escape persecution and oppression. It is unclear whether he had professed a faith.

Eventually, Matthew connected with twenty Egyptian construction workers in Sirte in northern Libya. The other men were Coptic Orthodox Christians, thirteen of them from the same small village. They were working to send money home to their families, including for their children's educations. One was saving up for his marriage.

The twenty-one men were kidnapped in Islamic State raids in December 2014 and January 2015. In February 2015, they were all dressed in orange jumpsuits and lined up on their knees to be beheaded for their Christian beliefs. Matthew, according to witnesses, was the last to be killed. His captors apparently were unsure as to his faith and offered him to spare him if he renounced Christ. Instead, he said, "Their God is my God," and was executed.

The remains of the Egyptians were returned in May 2018 and placed in a church built in the small hometown of many of the men. A year later, the Coptic Church requested Matthew's relics; he was interred in the Church in September 2020. No more information has come to light about his own roots or family or ambitions; some of the other martyrs' families now consider him a son or brother.

All the men were canonized in the Coptic Church the week after their executions. In May 2023, Pope Francis met with the head of the Coptic Orthodox Church and said in an address: "These martyrs were baptized not only in water and the Spirit, but also in blood, with a blood that is a seed of unity for all followers of Christ. I am pleased to announce today that, with your Holiness' consent, these twenty-one martyrs will be included in the Roman Martyrology as a sign of the spiritual communion uniting our two Churches."[14]

The martyrs were also remembered at an ecumenical prayer service on February 15, 2024, their first Catholic feast day.

A DEEPER DIVE

Was not the answer, "We are able," too bold? [James and John] knew neither what they asked nor what they promised; but just as their ignorant question was partly redeemed by its love, their ignorant vow was ennobled by its very rashness, as well as by the unfaltering love in it. They did not know what they were promising, but they knew that they loved him so well that to share anything with him would be blessed. So it was not in their own strength that the swift answer rushed to their lips, but in the strength of a love that makes heroes out of cowards. And they nobly redeemed their pledge. We, too, if we are Christ's, have the same question put to us, and, weak and timid as we are, may venture to give the same answer, trusting to his strength.

■ **ANDREW MACLAREN**, *Scottish Baptist minister, 1826–1910*[15]

John

THE ONE WHO LISTENED

DEATH: Traditionally, around 100 AD

FEAST DAY: December 27

SCRIPTURE: "I have other sheep that do not belong to this fold. I must bring them also, and they will listen to my voice. So there will be one flock, one shepherd. For this reason the Father loves me, because I lay down my life in order to take it up again."
■ **JOHN 10:16–17**

Who Was John?

John is identified as one of the Twelve in each synoptic gospel (Mark 3:17; Matthew 10:2; Luke 6:14). He is James's brother and one of the two "Sons of Thunder" as well as a son of Zebedee. Both John and James worked in their father's fishing business. John is generally believed to have been the younger of the brothers, and likely the youngest of the Twelve.

John was in Jesus' inner circle along with James and Peter. They are the only apostles at the healing of Jairus's daughter (Luke 8:41–42, 49–56; Mark 5:22–24, 35–43), the Transfiguration (Mark 9:2–13; Luke 9:28–36; Matthew 17:1–8), and the agony in the garden (Mark 14:33–42; Matthew 26:37–44).

The three of them and Peter's brother, Andrew, also are present when Jesus heals Peter's mother-in-law (Mark 1:29–31). They are with Jesus at the Mount of Olives when he says more about his foretelling of the temple's destruction (Mark 13:3–8).

John and James also are noteworthy in the synoptic gospels for their or their mother's brash request that they sit at Jesus' right and left in his kingdom (Mark 10:35–37; Matthew 20:20–21). A bit later, the brothers ask if they should "command fire to come down from heaven and consume" (Luke 9:54) Samaritans who didn't welcome messengers sent ahead of the followers, and are rebuked by Jesus.

John's name doesn't appear in the gospel that traditionally is credited to him. There is one reference to the sons of Zebedee being among those on Peter's fishing expedition where the men do not initially recognize the risen Lord (John 21:2).

It is tradition that this gospel's references to the apostle Jesus loved are about John. The beloved disciple is shown at the Last Supper, reclining close to Jesus' heart and learning who the betrayer will be (John 13:21–26). He is the only apostle who definitively was near the cross with the Marys. Jesus gives them to each other: "Woman, here is your son" (John 19:26) and "Here is your mother" (19:27). In John 20:1–9, we see the beloved disciple and Peter in a footrace to Jesus' tomb after Mary Magdalene reported that the stone had been removed. The beloved disciple gets there first but does not go in until after Peter, perhaps a sign of the acceptance of his role.

John appears with the others in Acts 1:13 at the coming of the Holy Spirit. Elsewhere in Acts, John and Peter are together when Peter heals a man with disabilities, and they both are called to account for the healing and their evangelization. The religious leaders recognize them as companions of Jesus due to their boldness and note they are "uneducated and ordinary men" (Acts 4:13). Peter and John also are sent to Samaria.

The details of John's later life are murky. According to tradition, he survived persecution and died of natural causes at Ephesus at an advanced age.

As to John authoring the gospel, the *New American Bible* (NAB) says that "most modern scholars find that the evidence does not support this"[16] but that there is a strong argument for it being an eyewitness account. While tradition connects John to the Book of Revelation, the NAB notes that the writer does not claim to be the apostle and that early Church fathers disagreed as to the author.[17] The NAB explains that scholars generally agree that the First Letter of John and the gospel were written by the same Johannine Christianity school due to their similarities in "style, vocabulary, and ideas"[18] and that the other two letters also likely had common authorship within that community.

Old Testament Scripture on **Listening**

1 SAMUEL 3:10
After repeated calls from the Lord and a conversation with Eli, Samuel responds to God, "Speak, for your servant is listening."

PSALM 68:33
The psalmist offers praise to God and urges the people: "listen, he sends out his voice, his mighty voice."

PROVERBS 8:34
Solomon advises that happiness is to be found listening to God, "watching daily at my gates, waiting besides my doors."

JOHN THE MAN

If John's story stopped at the Last Supper, we might be inclined to see him as a temperamental, even spoiled, young man. His father owns a fishing business that is successful enough that workers are hired. There is some thought that Zebedee served as high priest at times and that John is the other disciple who was known to the high priest at the time of Jesus' arrest. The other disciple goes into the high priest's courtyard with Jesus when Peter waits outside the gate, then is brought inside (John 18:15–16). Finally, John and James's mother may have been a sister or half-sister of the Blessed Virgin. It would appear that the sons of Zebedee had more standing in the community than the other followers.

While John and James together could be a challenging duo, John was no slouch in attempting to advance himself in Jesus' eyes. He reports that someone "who does not follow with us" was casting out demons in Jesus' name and that "we" had tried to stop him. Jesus says not to do that because "whoever is not against you is for you" (Luke 9:49–50; Mark 9:38–41).

But something changed in John. He started listening instead of pushing himself forward. He is at the cross with the Marys. It had to be a conversion moment to hear the suffering Jesus turn his mother over to John, and John to her.

Oh, to have been there that evening in John's home with the Blessed Virgin! Perhaps she shared all she had pondered in her heart the past thirty-four years. I would like to think that while she was devastated by her son's earthly end, she knew the story was not over and shared that with John. Maybe John then pondered in his heart all he had seen and heard in the past three or so years.

John's gospel is very different from the three synoptic gospels, which share the good news primarily in events, episodes, and parables. The fourth gospel does not include some significant events of Jesus' earthly ministry, such as the Transfiguration, the teaching of the Lord's Prayer, and the Sermon on the Mount. What it does include, and they are gloriously written, are Jesus' longer discourses, with notations that the apostles later realized the import of the Lord's words. That content in John's gospel could have only come from an eyewitness—one who listened to Jesus and was changed by him.

BEING JOHN TODAY

I believe God speaks to us more often than we acknowledge—through others, through signs, and sometimes even in words. But so often, we don't like what the Almighty says or are so twisted up about our own concerns that we don't listen.

It was a saint who truly opened my ears to the Lord, to the cloud of witnesses in heaven, and to the saints in the making here on earth.

A relics tour came to a parish near me in 2012 when I was writing a daily devotional on women saints. The priest who gave the introduction promised that a relic would speak to us. I got excited: Would it be St. Francis de Sales, the patron saint of writers? Would Teresa of Avila, the first female doctor of the Church, commune with me?

I wandered around, picking up relics in their holders. When I got to Elizabeth Ann Seton, the holder was noticeably warmer in my hand than the others. I waited.

"Listen, and you will find your vocation," the first native-born U.S. saint said.

There are all kinds of reasons why I love Elizabeth Ann Seton. Her national shrine and the place where she founded the first U.S. congregation of religious sisters is just seventy miles from where I live. The kindnesses that two of her husband's Catholic business associates showed her and a daughter after her husband's death in Italy spoke to her soul and led to her conversion. But I had never thought about her as a spiritual inspiration or guide for me as a writer or as a divorced and annulled, childless Catholic revert.

I kept the holder in my hand. She said it again: "Listen, and you will find your vocation."

I started relying less on my stack of books and pinned online resources about the women I was writing about. Yes, the facts are critical. But I pulled away from the screen and prayed with those women saints, asking them which of their stories they wanted me to tell. Listening made for a stronger book—and a better me. It makes me a better sister in Christ when I speak publicly and people come up to share their own stories afterward.

Listening is a gift, as John knew. It's what people generally need, not judgment and not problem solving. They know what that small, still voice is telling them. Often, they just need to say it out loud to understand what the Lord desires.

PONDERING LISTENING

- Read aloud John 10:16–17. How can you help bring sheep from outside the fold to Jesus? Think about your children, grandchildren, siblings, or other family members who are away from faith.
- It's hard, but people do change. In just three years or so, John went from a somewhat arrogant and entitled young man to the person to whom Jesus entrusted his mother and, later, the person with a community of followers who loved to hear his Jesus stories. Consider giving someone you've shut out of your life a second chance.
- Resolve to listen more than you speak in a difficult conversation today. Don't let evil drag you down the road of telling the person what to do unless he or she asks for your take on the situation.

JOHN IN IMAGES

Italian painter Simone Cantarini (1612–48) shows a very young apostle in *Saint John the Evangelist.*[19] John's right hand is on his heart. His eyes are closed or nearly so; perhaps he is reading the book he holds in his left hand or meditating on what he has just read. His red cloak is voluminous, with a black shirt showing underneath.

The apostle looks at peace and unhurried. How do you look during your prayer time? Do you immerse yourself in the Word, or do you think about your to-do list or work you must finish? Consider changing the location of your prayer time if your mind wanders.

Spanish painter Alonso Cano's (1601–67) *Saint John and the Poisoned Cup*[20] illustrates one tradition that John received a cup with poisoned wine; when he blessed the cup, the poison left it in the form of a snake. This reminds us of Jesus' warning that John and his brother would drink from the same cup as Jesus. John, whose face strongly resembles Jesus' in other paintings of the day, looks down at the snake and cup, his right hand raised. He is wearing a white garment with a light red cloak tossed over his left shoulder. From what we can see of his face, he is neither frightened nor jubilant.

When a "cup" you know is poisonous comes your way, what is your reaction? Do you retreat in fear? Become angry that you are in this situation? Consider employing prayer to help you remember that God's got this.

PRAYER

St. John, your stories and faith inspired your community of followers and continue to bless us today. Please help me to remember Jesus' words and incorporate them into the fiber of my being, as you did, so that I may evangelize within my community. Amen.

Another Who Listened

ST. MARIA ELIZABETH HESSELBLAD *(1870–1957)*

CANONIZED JUNE 5, 2016 ❧ FEAST DAY: JUNE 4

When Elizabeth (Maria in religious life) was born in Sweden, Catholics could face the death penalty or exile. It's likely she never met a Catholic until she moved to the United States at age eighteen to study nursing and help support her large, financially struggling family. The Lutheran Church of Sweden was the state religion until 2000.

Eventually, Elizabeth went to work for a Catholic family. The relationship became so close that she and the employers traveled around Europe together, including a visit with Elizabeth's family. Then, at a Brussels cathedral, she saw the Eucharist in a monstrance for the first time and had a conversion moment of sorts. It deepened when the group went to the site in Rome where St. Bridget of Sweden had spent her final years. Elizabeth was listening but was not yet sure what God wanted of her.

In 1902, one of her employer's daughters was entering the Visitation convent in Washington, DC. While there, Elizabeth encountered a Jesuit priest from the neighboring Georgetown University Observatory. That small, still voice told her this was the time. She immediately asked the priest to receive her into the Catholic faith. The two of them met twice a day for three days, with Elizabeth in retreat the remainder of the time. She was received into the Church three days later on the Feast of the Assumption and received her First Communion two days after that.

God was not done sharing plans with Elizabeth. She considered becoming a Carmelite, but poor health prevented that. Eventually, she felt called to become a sister of St. Bridget's community—the Order of the Most Holy Savior, or Brigidines—even though few sisters remained. She received a papal dispensation to do so and took the name Maria, then visited all of the community's remaining European convents. Laws regarding Catholics had changed in Sweden by then, and she eventually was able to reopen a convent in the town where St. Bridget's first monastery was located.

Maria's focus was on listening to people and bringing them together, saying, "The Lord has called us from different nations, but we must be united with one heart and one soul."[21] Her efforts toward ecumenical listening and mercy included housing at least a dozen Jews at the sisters' convent in Rome in the closing days of World War II.

A DEEPER DIVE

...let us be content here with learning an important lesson for our lives: the Lord wishes to make each one of us a disciple who lives in personal friendship with him. To achieve this, it is not enough to follow him and to listen to him outwardly: it is also necessary to live with him and like him. This is only possible in the context of a relationship of deep familiarity, imbued with the warmth of total trust. This is what happens between friends.

■ **POPE BENEDICT XVI**, *General Audience, July 5, 2006*[22]

Philip

THE INATTENTIVE ONE

DEATH: Late 1st century AD; possibly in Turkey

FEAST DAY: May 3 (with James son of Alphaeus)

SCRIPTURE: Philip said to him, "Lord, show us the Father, and we will be satisfied." ■ **JOHN 14:8**

Who Was Philip?

Philip is identified as one of the Twelve in each of the synoptic gospels (Mark 3:18; Matthew 10:3; Luke 6:14). He also appears with the others in Acts 1:13 at the coming of the Holy Spirit.

John's gospel provides much more insight into this apostle:

- After Jesus' call for Philip to follow him, Philip goes to Nathanael (Bartholomew), shares who Jesus is, and invites Nathanael to come and see as well (John 1:43–46).
- Philip responds to Jesus' question about where they could buy bread to feed the five thousand by saying six months' wages would not be sufficient for everyone in the crowd to get even a bit of bread (John 6:7).
- During Passover, some Greeks approach Philip and request an introduction to Jesus. Philip goes to Andrew, then the two of them go to Jesus. Jesus announces that his hour has come (John 12:20–23).
- At the Last Supper, Philip tells Jesus to show them the Father "and we will be satisfied" and is rebuked by Jesus (John 14:8–10).

We know Philip was from Bethsaida and knew Andrew and Peter; we can infer that he knew John and James. He also may have been one of the unnamed disciples in the group who didn't initially recognize the risen Lord when they go fishing (John 21:2). While none of the gospels specifically says so, Philip, like Andrew, is believed to have been a follower of St. John the Baptist.

The name Philip is Greek, meaning "lover of horses," and it appears the apostle spoke Greek.

The Acts accounts of a man named Philip evangelizing in Samaria refer to St. Philip the Evangelist, not the apostle. Some early historians seem to have confused the two. Philip the Evangelist was one of the seven men the apostles chose (Acts 6:5) to minister to the Church in Jerusalem who then went on to a robust ministry elsewhere.

Philip the Apostle appears to have preached in Scythia in Eurasia. He may have been crucified or beheaded in Turkey. His relics and those of St. James son of Alphaeus, with whom Philip shares a feast day, reside in the Basilica of the Twelve Holy Apostles in Rome. A relic of Philip is housed at a church in upstate New York as well.[23]

Old Testament Scripture on **Attentiveness**

DEUTERONOMY 31:6
As Moses names Joshua as his successor, Moses reminds the Israelites to be strong and bold because God will not forsake them.

1 SAMUEL 3:10
Samuel follows Eli's counsel when the Lord calls to Samuel a third time, saying, "Speak, for your servant is listening."

PSALM 81:8–14
Through the psalmist, God tells the people how much easier their lives would be if they listened to him.

PHILIP THE MAN

Philip started out attentive enough. Not only does he follow immediately when Jesus calls him, he tells his friend Nathanael and shares that the Messiah has been found. When Nathanael doubts, Philip says, "Come and see" (John 1:46).

But after that, Philip becomes the logistics guy, the one who doesn't see the big picture. You know people like Philip. You may be like Philip, analyzing the details of the problem at hand rather than thinking about the goal.

At the feeding of the five thousand, when Jesus saw the crowd approaching, he tested Philip by asking, "Where are we to buy bread for these people to eat?" (John 6:6). This could indicate that Jesus had experience with Philip's inattentiveness to situations and indeed to the Lord himself. Philip's response shows that gap in his faith. He tells Jesus that even if they had the equivalent of 200 days' wages, they couldn't buy enough bread for everyone to get a taste.

Jesus did not ask Philip how much money the ministry had or how much money would be needed. He asked where bread could be purchased. Maybe the response Jesus desired was something along the lines of "I don't know, Rabbi. Where could we get that much bread?"

Later, after the triumphal entry into Jerusalem, some people approach Philip, asking to meet with Jesus. They are described as "Greeks," but it is thought that this is meant to symbolize Gentile converts. The term also may refer to Hellenistic Jews. Galileans typically were bilingual, and the group may have heard Philip's name, which is Greek, and decided to approach him.

But Philip doesn't take the Greeks to Jesus. He tells Andrew, a fellow Galilean, the guy who is forever introducing people to Jesus. Philip misses the import of this possible evangelization opportunity, seeing it instead as a matter of access, and providing access to Jesus is not something we've seen Philip do since he invited Nathanael to come and see. Together, Philip and Andrew go to the Lord, and it is to them—not Peter, not James, not John—that Jesus reveals that his hour has come.

Soon thereafter at the Last Supper, Jesus has done and said several bewildering things. He has washed the disciples' feet. He has predicted that he will be betrayed by one of them that very evening. He has said that Peter will deny him three times in a matter of hours. He has said that he will be with them only a little longer and that they cannot immediately follow where he is going. He has answered Thomas's question about how they will know the way to this new, unknown place: "If you know me, you will know my Father also. From now on you do know him and have seen him" (John 14:7).

Let's give Philip some grace and assume he is so frightened and confused that he wasn't paying attention to Jesus' response to Thomas. Immediately thereafter, Philip says, "Lord, show us the Father, and we will be satisfied" (John 14:8). You can almost see the Son of God go slack-jawed. Has Jesus ever said his goal on earth is to do acts that will "satisfy" his followers?

His response is close to a rebuke: "Have I been with you all this time, Philip, and you still do not know me? Whoever has seen me has seen the Father. How can you say, 'Show us the Father'? Do you not believe that I am in the Father and the Father is in me?" (John 14:9–10).

Mercifully, we do not see or hear Philip's response.

BEING PHILIP TODAY

For most of my life, I considered myself a good editor. I prided myself on being able to tighten prose to make it more accessible to readers while not disturbing the writer's voice. I was an OK writer, but nothing special.

I spent a long time ignoring God's nudges that I should write. Writing doesn't pay as well as editing, and for many years, I needed the extra income. Then a good friend talked me into writing a daily devotional with her. A publisher didn't want that manuscript but asked us if we would write a daily devotional on women saints. My friend wasn't interested, but I was intrigued. Were there really that many women saints? I cried when I finished the manuscript, grateful for the way God had introduced the women to me. But I still didn't consider myself a writer.

About half a dozen Catholic non-fiction books followed. But there was this Christian-not-Catholic novel languishing in my computer. When I retired from my day job, I decided to enter it in a prestigious contest for unpublished fiction writers. I semifinaled in my category, which discomforted me more than it excited me. I spent a lot of time coming up with all the reasons God didn't want this: I'm too old. I'm a mid-list Catholic non-fiction author. My social media life by choice has all but dried up since 2020.

Finally, after a non-writer friend said it sounded like I was too prideful to pay attention to God's plan, I went to the conference where the fiction contest winners would be announced. I didn't final, but I made some new friends. The publishing house I really wanted to work with wasn't interested in that novel, but the editor I met with was encouraging about my skill and asked to see another novel I was writing when it was ready.

I started working on that novel a couple of hours a day and joined a large online critique group. But then my friends at Twenty-Third Publications asked what I was interested in writing next. I shared an idea that had been on my heart and ended up with a contract for the book you're reading now.

Funny how when you pay attention to what God desires of you, the cross that seemed so heavy becomes lighter.

PONDERING ATTENTIVENESS

- Read John 14:8 aloud. Where are you commanding Jesus to do something that will "satisfy" you? Maybe you want to know why a loved one has died; why you suffer in body, mind, or spirit; or why the world is so chaotic. Think about why you expect an earthly explanation from the Almighty.
- Someone is reaching out to you to learn more about Jesus. Perhaps they're intrigued by what they've seen on a livestream or in a theater. Do you tell them to read the Bible or the *Catechism of the Catholic Church*, listen to a podcast, or schedule an appointment with a priest—or do you listen and introduce them to the ways the Lord is working in your life?
- Write out in longhand—printing or cursive will do—your favorite prayer or Bible verse. Then contemplate it, considering the power and purpose of each word rather than rushing through because you have other obligations that seem more important than prayer.

PHILIP IN IMAGES

The Triumphal Arch at the Basilica of San Vitale in Ravenna, Italy, features beautiful mosaics of the apostles and others. Philip is depicted as a dark-haired, long-faced man with a short beard and piercing brown eyes.[24]

Consider Philip's ears in the mosaic. Do they seem a bit outsized compared with the rest of his face? Perhaps the creator was emphasizing the importance of keeping our ears open to better listen to the Lord. Where are you consciously or unconsciously closing your ears?

In the famed Apostles Series of paintings by Peter Paul Rubens (1577–1640) housed at the Prado in Madrid,[25] Philip is the only apostle depicted gazing at a cross.

During his time with Jesus on earth, Philip sometimes lost sight of the gift right in front of him—Jesus. Consider the times that you let everyday life take your eyes off the Lord's desires and plans for you. How can you refocus on your cross, pick it up daily, and follow?

PRAYER

St. Philip, sometimes I forget that those two greatest commandments are to be lived daily and humbly. I figure I'm all right because I have chosen to follow the Lord and do all the sacramental things. Please show me how to listen and live my faith daily despite all the world's noise. Amen.

Another Whose Attentiveness Grew
ST. ÓSCAR ROMERO *(1917–80)*

CANONIZED OCTOBER 14, 2018 FEAST DAY: MARCH 24

When he was named archbishop of San Salvador in 1977, Óscar had been a priest for nearly thirty-five years. It wasn't that he had trouble paying attention to God, but some thought he could have paid more attention to God's people. El Salvador was on the verge of civil war, and Óscar was seen as a social conservative or traditionalist.

But something happened to get his attention. Less than a month after his installation as archbishop, his good friend Rutilio Grande, a Jesuit priest, was assassinated by Salvadoran security forces. The precipitating incident may have been a fiery homily Rutilio preached a few weeks earlier about the Salvadoran government's expulsion of a Colombian priest who had been kidnapped by guerillas and then released.

After his friend's death, Óscar became an outspoken critic of the ruling junta and its persecution of the poor and others. He was assassinated himself three years later while offering Mass at a Carmelite sisters' hospital in San Salvador. To this day, no one has been convicted in his slaying.

A DEEPER DIVE

Let us conclude our reflection by recalling the aim to which our whole life must aspire: to encounter Jesus as Philip encountered him, seeking to perceive in him God himself, the heavenly Father. If this commitment were lacking, we would be reflected back to ourselves as in a mirror and become more and more lonely! Philip teaches us instead to let ourselves be won over by Jesus, to be with him and also to invite others to share in this indispensable company; and in seeing, finding God, to find true life.

■ **POPE BENEDICT XVI,** *General Audience, September 6, 2006*[26]

Bartholomew Nathanael

THE ONE WHO ASSUMED

DEATH: Traditionally, around 69–71 AD

FEAST DAY: August 24

SCRIPTURE: Nathanael said to [Philip], "Can anything good come out of Nazareth?" ■ **JOHN 1:46**

Who Was Nathanael?

This apostle is generally believed to be the same person as the apostle Bartholomew. Bartholomew is found in the lists of apostles in all three synoptic gospels (Matthew 10:3; Mark 3:18; Luke 6:14). He also appears with the others in Acts 1:13 at the coming of the Holy Spirit. The synoptic gospels do not refer to Nathanael.

John's gospel does not refer to Bartholomew. However, the apostle Nathanael appears twice. He is among those who don't initially recognize the risen Lord when they go fishing (John 21:2); more importantly, he exhibits an almost dismissive attitude when Philip tells him about Jesus (John 1:45–49).

This chapter uses the name Nathanael for study purposes because of John's rich scene.

Nathanael was from Cana and so likely was at the wedding with other followers when Jesus turned water into wine. We don't know where he or most of the apostles were as Jesus was crucified; they may have been among the acquaintances Luke 23:49 says were standing at a distance.

Ancient writings indicate he evangelized in India and, possibly with the apostle Jude Thaddeus, in Armenia. Legends of his martyrdom vary but all are horrific: crucified; kidnapped, beaten, and cast into the sea to drown; or flayed and beheaded.

NATHANAEL THE MAN

Imagine the apostle Philip's excitement. Tradition tells us he may have been among those who heard John the Baptist call this Jesus of Nazareth "the Lamb of God who takes away the sin of the world" (John 1:29). Philip's friends Andrew and Peter have dropped everything to follow Jesus, and now Jesus has called him to follow as well! What could be more natural than to share this news with his friend Nathanael?

Nathanael, however, is considerably less excited. "Can anything good come out of Nazareth?" he responds.

We're not sure where Nathanael's hometown of Cana is today. Archeological digs seem to indicate it is most likely Khribet Qana, a community of about 20,000 people located eight miles southeast of Nazareth. Another possible contender is Kar Kanna, less than five miles northeast of Nazareth.

Regardless, the town was close to Nazareth and was no major hub of activity itself. But Nazareth? As the eighteenth-century Puritan theologian John Gill put it:

Old Testament Scripture on **Assumptions**

ISAIAH 55:8–9
God reminds the people that his thoughts and ways are higher than theirs.

JOB 38:1–41
Speaking out of a whirlwind, God challenges Job's understanding of the Almighty's power.

PSALM 27:14
David emphasizes the importance of waiting for the Lord.

> The whole country of Galilee was [held] in contempt with the Jews; but Nazareth was so mean a place, that it seems it was even despised by its neighbors, by the Galileans themselves....It was so miserable a place that [Nathanael] could hardly think that any sort of good thing, even any worldly good thing, could come from thence....[27]

But this was more than civic rivalry. Nathanael was also making assumptions about the Messiah, assumptions that seemed to be well founded but weren't because he didn't have the full picture. Take, for example, Micah 5:2, in which the prophet says the ruler of the Israelites would come from Bethlehem. Nathanael didn't know Jesus had been born there. Then there was Hosea 11:1, which states that God's Son would be called "out of Egypt," where Jesus spent part of his childhood.

But Philip doesn't turn away from Nathanael after those words of prejudice and assumption. Come and see, he says. And then Nathanael's conversion begins.

Upon seeing Nathanael, Jesus says, "Here is truly an Israelite in whom there is no deceit!" (John 1:47). Nathanael asks how Jesus knows him. The Lord answers that he saw Nathanael under the fig tree before Philip called him.

Where was the fig tree, and why does it matter? Some scholars believe Nathanael was praying or reading under the tree, possibly at his own home. Some believe that contemplation included Jacob's dream of a stairway to heaven. But Jesus knew what Nathanael had been doing and chose this way to show Nathanael he was more than just a man from Nazareth.

To Nathanael, that's all it takes. "Rabbi, you are the Son of God! You are the King of Israel!" (John 1:49) he replies. Jesus says Nathanael will see much greater things, including "heaven opened and the angels of God ascending and descending upon the Son of Man" (John 1:51), a possible reference to Genesis 28:12.

It's the last we see of Nathanael until after Jesus' resurrection. In some ways, this first interaction with Jesus reminds us of one of the gospels' most moving conversions, that of the Samaritan woman at the well in John 4. And perhaps that's the greatest lesson Nathanael's call provides: Jesus knows us and doesn't turn away from our flaws because he believes in our capacity to become the person he desires—if we follow.

BEING NATHANAEL TODAY

I heard about Colleen at our parish for a couple of years before we met. Someone at coffee and doughnuts after Mass regularly mused about how I was from South Dakota and Colleen was from North Dakota. I made an immediate assumption: I mean, North Dakota. Why would I want to meet someone simply because she was from North Dakota?

Then I got involved in a lay Catholic movement, one to which she and her husband were dedicated—it's how they met. The group had a retreat, and I finally got to meet her, sort of. She kept withdrawing to the room she was sharing with her husband or going outside to talk on her phone. I got into a couple of good conversations with her husband, though. I was working on a novel that involved a hunting storyline, and he knew a lot about deer hunting in the area as well as the benefits and drawbacks of using a rifle, shotgun, or bow and arrow. He was easy to talk with. I decided Colleen was kind of snotty.

Then the two of us ended up in leadership roles in the local group. I was doing the communications part, including a sorely needed website overhaul, and some of the previous owners were withholding information and sandbagging me at meetings. I handled it poorly. Colleen decided being around me was a near occasion of sin and told the president she would no longer attend meetings where I was present.

Then, one Saturday evening at Mass, a mutual friend told me she was going to be on the group's weekend retreat team for women interested in learning more about deepening their relationship with Jesus and community. I asked her who was in charge. She said Colleen. Good luck with that, I thought.

At home, I got a phone call inviting me to be on the same team. My only other experience of being on a team had not gone well. I had reacted poorly to what I saw as chaos and a lack of leadership. I decided, Colleen or no Colleen, I needed to give this another try.

Meanwhile, Colleen found out I was going to be on the team. She wasn't excited, but she didn't stamp her feet and refuse either. She says she figured the Holy Spirit had something in mind.

And indeed, the Holy Spirit did have something in mind. During team formation, we learned that those assumptions we'd made about each other were entirely wrong, mainly because we didn't know about personal crises we each were going through. Fifteen years and many prayer requests, family and personal challenges, collaborative projects, dinners, and glasses of wine later, we have established one of the deepest friendships I've ever had. One of the many things our relationship has taught me is that we never know what's going on in someone else's life, and we need to attempt to accept and love them as they are, just as Jesus does.

PONDERING ASSUMPTIONS

- Read aloud John 1:46. Where are you underestimating the Lord's presence in your world, and how might you change that?
- That person who works your last nerve in your parish or in your neighborhood or at work: How can God possibly love

them as much as you? Doesn't the Almighty see the way they fall asleep during Mass, monopolize association meetings, or try to take all the credit for projects? Pray that your eyes be opened to see what God loves about them.

- Take a deep breath, then reach out to a family member or friend whom you love but have been avoiding because of heated discussions about politics or some other issue. Invite the person to coffee or lunch, with the condition that that topic is off limits. Rediscover the joys you share.

NATHANAEL IN IMAGES

In this black-and-white illustration,[28] Nathanael appears a bit unconvinced, seated as his friend Philip stands and extends his left arm, presumably pointing out Jesus, who is not seen. The illustration by W.J. Morgan (1847–1924) appears in *The Bible and Its Story, Taught by One Thousand Picture Lessons* (1910).

Consider Nathanael's position. His head isn't even turned to the direction of Philip's hand; he's looking straight ahead. Is someone trying to show you Jesus in a new way, but you're having trouble accepting that? Give your friend—and Jesus—a chance. Look.

In one of the least gruesome depictions of Nathanael's martyrdom, Flemish painter Peter Paul Rubens (1577–1640), in *St. Bartholomew*, shows an aged apostle, nearly bald, holding a knife.[29] The knife signifies the tradition that Nathanael's skin was stripped from his body.

Notice the detail work on Nathanael's fingers, the neatly trimmed nails, and the positioning of his left hand over his heart. His eyes gaze at something we don't see. Is it his torturer? Jesus?

PRAYER

St. Nathanael, I too often make assumptions, good and bad, about people. Intercede for me, that I might love as God loves and meet people where they are today, not where I think they should be. Amen.

Another Who Made Assumptions

ST. IRMÃ DULCE LOPES PONTES *(1914–92)*

CANONIZED OCTOBER 13, 2019 FEAST DAY: AUGUST 13

Dulce's assumptions were quite different from Nathanael's. She assumed that God loves everyone, and therefore everyone was deserving of her love and help.

She grew up in northeast Brazil in an upper-middle-class family. Her mother died when Dulce was six years old, and the extended family took an active role in raising the children. Her father, a dentist and professor, was known for his acts of charity.

One day, an aunt took Dulce to a poor area of their hometown. It isn't known what specifically the thirteen-year-old saw, but it prompted her to action. She started bringing people to the family home to provide them with care.

At eighteen, she entered the Congregation of the Missionary Sisters of the Immaculate Conception, taking her mother's name, Dulce, as hers in religious life. Her acts of charity included establishing an orphanage and care center, a clinic for the poor, a school for working families, and a workers' organization. In her thirties, the neighborhood where she set up housekeeping with seventy sick people kicked the household out. The same thing happened when Dulce moved with the group to an old fish market. Finally, her mother superior gave her permission to use the community's chicken coop—with the provision Dulce would care for the chickens. She turned them into meals for the others.

Dulce would roam the streets at night, looking for people who needed medical care but couldn't afford it. Near the end of her life, even when her lung capacity was diminished, she would physically carry people to the hospital.

Her life included two Nobel Peace Prize nominations and two personal audiences with St. John Paul II. She was honored after her death as Brazil's most admired woman ever and her country's most influential religious person of the twentieth century.

A DEEPER DIVE

Nathanael's words shed light on a twofold, complementary aspect of Jesus' identity: he is recognized both in his special relationship with God the Father, of whom he is the Only-begotten Son, and in his relationship with the People of Israel, of whom he is the declared King, precisely the description of the awaited Messiah. We must never lose sight of either of these two elements because if we only proclaim Jesus' heavenly dimension, we risk making him an ethereal and evanescent being; and if, on the contrary, we recognize only his concrete place in history, we end by neglecting the divine dimension that properly qualifies him.

■ **POPE BENEDICT XVI**, *General Audience, October 4, 2006*[30]

Thomas

THE ONE WHO STRUGGLED

DEATH: Traditionally, 72 AD in India

FEAST DAY: July 3

SCRIPTURE: [Jesus] said to Thomas, "Put your finger here and see my hands. Reach out your hand and put it in my side. Do not doubt but believe." Thomas answered him, "My Lord and my God!"
■ **JOHN 20:27–28**

Who Was Thomas?

Thomas is identified as one of the Twelve in each of the synoptic gospels (Mark 3:18; Matthew 10:3; Luke 6:15). He also appears with the others in Acts 1:13 in the coming of the Holy Spirit.

John's gospel provides much more insight into this apostle:

- Thomas's declaration that the disciples should accompany Jesus and journey to see Lazarus after Lazarus's death "that we may die with him" (John 11:16).
- His statement to Jesus at the Last Supper that they don't know where the Lord is going (John 14:5).
- Thomas's absence when Jesus appears to the disciples in a group after the resurrection and his awe when Jesus returns a week later (John 20:24–29).
- Thomas's presence among the seven disciples who don't initially recognize the risen Lord when they go fishing (John 21:2).

Church tradition holds that Thomas was from Galilee. His trade is not known, nor is the reason that John's gospel refers to Thomas three times as "the twin" or Didymus. (We do know that his name translates as "twin.")

It is believed Thomas's post-Pentecost assignment included India, where he evangelized for many years until his martyrdom in about 72 AD, possibly by a spear. Santhome Cathedral Basilica[31] on India's southeast coast, which tradition holds was erected over Thomas's grave, is visited by more than 200,000 people annually. In 1986, St. John Paul II became the first pope to visit the basilica.

According to Catholics India,[32] more than 21 million baptized Catholics, or about 1.67 percent of the population, live in India today. Those who follow Hinduism make up most of the population (about 80 percent).

Old Testament Scripture on **Struggle**

GENESIS 32:24–30
Jacob struggles with an agent of God all night, refusing to let go until he has been blessed.

ISAIAH 41:8–13
God reminds the Israelites of Jacob's story and reminds them he holds their right hands and will help them.

PSALM 27:14
David urges patience and courage in waiting for the Lord's goodness to become evident.

THOMAS THE MAN

"If your mother says she loves you, check it out."

From 1890 to 2005, Chicago was home to the City News Bureau, an independent news organization that was kind of a hyper-local version of today's Associated Press, Bloomberg, or Reuters wire services. Many famous writers started out at City News.

The run-down office had a big banner: "If your mother says she loves you, check it out." Because back in the day, that's what journalists did, and not just at City News. They had to get two sources, generally willing to be identified by name, before any story could go public.

The apostle Thomas would have made a great journalist—and he made a great evangelist, perhaps because of his willingness to ask questions, even when it made him look like less than a true believer.

Surely, Thomas wasn't the only one of the Twelve who wasn't clear where Jesus was going after the Last Supper and how the apostles would get there without him. (Later in the passage, Philip shows perhaps even more obtuseness.) But Thomas is the first to put his struggle into words. He asks Jesus for an explanation on the spot, not waiting to ask the others what they thought the Lord meant. There's a certain trust in taking that struggle public, including the risk of eye rolling by his companions.

When Jesus was more literal, Thomas was more comfortable. Not long before Passover, Jesus waits when he is informed his friend Lazarus is ill. Two days later, Jesus says Lazarus is dead, and it's time to go to him in Bethany. Thomas doesn't ask about the timing. Instead, he echoes Jesus' words about going but adds what he anticipates will happen: "that we may die with him." He reads into Jesus' words something that was not there.

Thomas's big scenes come after Jesus rises from the dead. He's not with the others when Jesus appears after the resurrection. The followers are in a locked room, fearful for their safety. When Jesus appears, he literally shows them his hands and his side. Small wonder that they believe! And that's all Thomas asks—to have the same experience.

I imagine Thomas not so much as a doubter but as someone struggling with his place in this new group dynamic. Why did Jesus come while he was gone? Why didn't the Lord wait until everyone was together? Thomas may have gone out for water or food or some other necessity. Maybe he was helping a member of the community who was more secretive about his or her faith, or maybe he was assisting a family member. Given that the room was locked, this errand could have involved some peril to Thomas, but he undertook it anyway. And missing Jesus is his thanks? Who wouldn't have been upset?

Thomas gets to stew about the injustice of it all for an entire week. That's right, seven days of the others likely talking about nothing other than Jesus' visit, leaving Thomas feeling different, less valued, less important. Then Jesus returns. He speaks directly to Thomas, offering his hands and side, and provides a short but powerful lesson. It's not a rebuke exactly, but he tells Thomas to believe, not doubt.

And Thomas provides the only answer any person yearning for faith could: "My Lord and my God!"

BEING THOMAS TODAY

Questions. I had questions. I was contemplating a return to the Catholic Church after thirty-three years. Nothing was working in my life, and the people around me who were serene about challenges worse than mine all had one thing in common: Christ. I tried a few Protestant churches, but after a few months I realized that only Catholicism would work for me. I believed in the True Presence. But I wasn't coming back without knowing exactly what the requirements were.

I signed up at a nearby parish for an eight-week course where those considering a return could ask questions. I bought a copy of the *Catechism of the Catholic Church* and looked up Church teachings on everything I had questions on: the role of women; limbo; divorce; purgatory; and of course, heaven and hell, as I had committed so many sins I truly wasn't sure God wanted me. I didn't read every page of the *Catechism*. But reading a good share of it convinced me that I hadn't truly understood the Church I had left just before my sixteenth birthday and that even the teachings I found difficult were based in love. It also convinced me that for whatever reason, God loved me.

Then, in January 2006, a whole month after my full re-communion with the Catholic Church, I ended up on the parish council. I came up with a whole new set of questions. Why not ask them than during council meetings instead of listening to those boring ministry reports?

Why was the place where things are needed for the consecration called a credence table? What was an ambo, and why couldn't I read the parish announcements at the end of Mass from there? What was the difference between a ciborium and the tabernacle?

Then there was the profound stuff, like what did it mean when someone called Christians "a Resurrection people" or said that people—not just Jesus, but all of us—have to go through the crucifixion before the resurrection.

It would have been easier for everyone if the pastor or council president had gently suggested I ask those questions another time, or that I consult my catechism or search engine, or perhaps suggested that I return to council in a year. I certainly would have felt relieved.

But they didn't. With patience and love, they answered my questions. Several council members took me to coffee or dinner individually, asked about my struggles, and shared their own and how God had helped them.

The pastor and the council president are both dead now, and many of the other council members have moved on to other parishes and cities. The ones I still know just give a laugh and a smile when we talk about those days. And I thank them—for emptying themselves and for seeing that I had enough baby faith to bring those doubts and struggles into the light instead of just giving up the struggle.

PONDERING STRUGGLE

- Read aloud John 20:19–20, the risen Lord's appearance to the disciples. Picture their shift from fearful to jubilant as Jesus shows them his hands and side. Then put yourself in Thomas's place. Think about a time when all the cool kids were raving about a homily, religious gathering, or faith-based movie or show and you felt left out. Did you rejoice at their joy, or did you hold back or denigrate their words because you felt excluded?
- In John 11:11–16, Jesus says Lazarus is dead, and the group will go to him. Thomas assumes this spells the earthly end of the apostles and appears to embrace that. It's somewhat reminiscent of when Jesus told Francis of Assisi to "rebuild my church" and Francis heard "repair the physical plant" rather than repair the body of Christ. Think of a time when you misinterpreted God's desires and made your life harder. What are some ways to keep that from happening again?
- There is a Thomas in your life. Maybe it's a child or grandchild, or someone on a ministry committee or at work who has to ask questions about everything you're trying to do. Just for today, assume noble intent and believe that the questions are being asked because the person is struggling, not trying to annoy you. Respond as Jesus would.

THOMAS'S STRUGGLE IN IMAGES

It is perhaps the best-known painting of Thomas's encounter with the risen Jesus. The Italian painter Caravaggio (1571–1610)'s *The Incredulity of Saint Thomas*[33] has as its focal point Thomas inserting a finger into Jesus' right side. Jesus guides Thomas's finger to the spot. Two others, presumed to be Peter and John, look on.

Where is your doubt today? Perhaps you despair of a loved one ever returning to faith or are having trouble accepting the loss of a friend or family member or your own medical condition. Where is Jesus guiding your hand and heart to quell your struggle?

Flemish painter Peter Paul Rubens (1577–1640), in *Martyrdom of St. Thomas*,[34] depicts Thomas dressed in black and under attack by a man with a spear and another man poised to throw a stone; a third has a dagger pointed toward Thomas's throat. Thomas's right arm reaches out to a group of angels above.

What influences are threatening your faith? Maybe it's people who deride you for your beliefs, or maybe it's your own doubts. The angels and Jesus are always near; how might you reach out to them for relief?

PRAYER

St. Thomas, free me from my private doubts and fears. May I follow your example and not fear sharing my struggle. Please help me to find the answers to my struggles in Scripture, Sacred Tradition, prayer, and community. Please intercede for me, that I may give voice to my struggles in conversation with a spiritual director, priest, or trusted friend. Amen.

Another Who Struggled

ST. MARIAM THRESIA CHIRAMEL MANKIDIYAN

(1876–1926)

CANONIZED OCTOBER 13, 2019 · FEAST DAY: JUNE 6

Her parents named her Teresa for St. Teresa of Ávila, but when she was in her twenties, she began going by Mariam due to her devotion to the Blessed Virgin Mary. She was born in a town about 400 miles west of where St. Thomas is believed to be buried and was raised as a Syro-Malabar Catholic. (That Eastern Catholic Church is in full communion with Rome.)

At almost every turn, Mariam's life was marked by struggle. Her mother died when she was twelve, and her father drowned in alcohol his extended family's descent from wealth to poverty. Mariam was met with criticism in her teens when she and three friends went into the streets to nurse underprivileged people at a time when proper women did not leave home without a male chaperone.

Around this time, she began receiving ecstasies, visions, and stigmata. The most intense came between 1902 and 1905, when she underwent three exorcisms. It is unclear how much occurred due to a sort of mental health issue rather than demons.

Mariam also met with barriers when she wanted to form a community with her friends that would be a house of prayer for them and a vehicle for helping those who struggled financially or physically. After ten years of tests and trials, her bishop agreed. It took only one more year before he saw the value of the institution and established the Congregation of the Holy Family, with Mariam as its first superior.

Mariam died just twelve years later: her last recorded words were "love one another and help one another."[35] Today, nearly 2,000 of her sisters do just that in more than 250 convents in India.

A DEEPER DIVE

As we touch those brothers and sisters with tenderness, we welcome the living God in our midst. Like St. Thomas, we look at the wounds of Jesus, which had stunned the disciples and could have thrown them into a hopeless guilt, and see that it is from those wounds the Lord made channels of forgiveness and mercy....What amazement must have seized the apostle Thomas as he contemplated them and saw his doubts and fears vanish before the greatness of God!

■ **POPE FRANCIS**, *Address to Syro-Malabar Church members, May 13, 2024*[36]

Matthew

THE OUTSIDER

DEATH: Unknown

FEAST DAY: September 21

SCRIPTURE: As Jesus was walking along, he saw a man called Matthew sitting at the tax-collection station, and he said to him, "Follow me." And he got up and followed him. ■ **MATTHEW 9:9**

Who Was Matthew?

Matthew is identified as one of the Twelve in each of the synoptic gospels (Mark 3:18; Matthew 10:3; Luke 6:15). In the chapter before Matthew lists the apostles, he describes his own call (9:9); that verse is soon followed by the Pharisees challenging the disciples for Jesus' eating with tax collectors and sinners at Matthew's home. Mark 2:13–17 and Luke 5:27–32 describe the call and the dinner similarly, but Luke calls the apostle "Levi"; Mark refers to him as "Levi son of Alphaeus." The *Catholic Encyclopedia* says it is not unusual that this man would have two names and that Jesus likely gave him the name Matthew; the same source also notes it is likely Matthew was born in Galilee.[37]

The fathers of both Matthew and James the Less are listed as Alphaeus. While their fathers may be the same man, many scholars note that the gospels identify Peter and Andrew as brothers, and James the Greater and John are identified as the sons of Zebedee. It seems unlikely that if Matthew and James the Less were brothers, that would not have been noted.

Matthew is not mentioned in John's gospel.

We don't know where he or most of the apostles were as Jesus was crucified; they may have been among the acquaintances Luke 23:49 says were standing at a distance.

Matthew also appears with the others in Acts 1:13 at the coming of the Holy Spirit.

Tradition holds that the apostle wrote the Gospel of Matthew and that it was the first of the four to be written. However, the *New American Bible* introduction to this gospel says that authorship is "untenable"[38] because so much of the work is based on Mark's gospel. The introduction adds that Matthew may have been responsible for some of the traditions in that gospel, "but that is far from certain."

Where Matthew evangelized is unclear. Most early writers indicate his ministry included what is today Armenia. While the Church considers him to have died as a martyr, the circumstances, place, and year of his death are unknown.

Old Testament Scripture on **Outsiders**

PSALM 119:141

The psalmist acknowledges he is "small and despised" but remembers God's precepts.

2 MACCABEES 1:27

The author's letter asks God to "look on those who are rejected and despised."

ZEPHANIAH 3:19

Through the prophet, God promises to "gather the outcast" and "change their shame into praise...."

MATTHEW THE MAN

I worked for the U.S. Department of the Treasury's Bureau of the Fiscal Service for about ten years. It is an important yet unknown agency, disbursing more than $5 billion in government payments like Social Security and processing a similar amount in payments to the federal government, such as National Park Service fees, each year. When people asked where I worked, I would just say something like "A little bureau of the Department of the Treasury you've never heard of—not the Internal Revenue Service!"

While I was at the bureau, I worked very closely with the IRS, and for a two-year project often traveled with my IRS colleagues. They always told people they worked for Treasury, never IRS. These men and women were passionate public servants. But they knew people's typical reaction to IRS employees.

I wonder what Matthew said when strangers asked about his occupation. Maybe there weren't that many strangers who came through Capernaum. And surely, nearly all the 1,500 or so residents knew who and what the guy in the tax collection booth was.

The Romans pretty much ignored him other than when he remitted the money he was supposed to collect on the empire's behalf: import and export duties, merchant licensing fees, a levy on what the merchants sold in town, and the like. As long as Rome got its due, the government couldn't have cared less how much Matthew charged people.

The typical tax collectors didn't just collect enough to cover the payment to Rome and a modest living for themselves. They were at liberty to charge however much they wanted. We get a hint of Matthew's philosophy on that topic after he follows Jesus and, according to Luke 5:29, gives "a great banquet for [Jesus] in his house."

Other than Jesus' followers (and they likely came reluctantly), the average Jewish resident wouldn't have entered a tax collector's home. They probably shunned him if they passed in the street. It's also likely a given that the Pharisees and scribes who complained about the gala didn't come inside. Tax collectors like Matthew were so despised by the Pharisees that they were sometimes banned from the synagogue. So, the only friends Matthew would have had would have been people just like him—outcasts.

Matthew had probably seen Jesus and his ragtag band of followers around. Some of them may have even owed him money. But Jesus didn't castigate Matthew for his sins, or even say hello. He said only two words: "Follow me." And something in Matthew's hard exterior broke with that invitation. He left his collection station. We can imagine the stunned look on those in line to make payments.

Matthew offered the only type of thanks he knew. He threw a great feast, and besides Jesus, no doubt invited all his friends: other tax collectors and sinners. He must have marveled when the Pharisees and their scribes complained to Jesus and the Lord answered, "Those who are well have no need of a physician, but those who are sick. Go and learn what this means, 'I desire mercy, not sacrifice.' For I have not come to call the righteous but sinners" (Matthew 9:12–13).

I like to think the other disciples were moved by his conversion and accepted him as a brother in Christ. But even if they didn't, Matthew was no longer an outsider. He was redeemed and claimed.

BEING MATTHEW TODAY

I hung out with Marla nearly every day in the summer after eighth grade. We'd known each other from classes for a couple of years, but that summer we really clicked. We rode bikes, went to movies and the public swimming pool, and participated in library summer reading groups.

Things changed in the fall. Marla made some older friends and started smoking and drinking and wearing way too much eyeliner. She became a Bad Girl, and there was no room in my life for Bad Girls. When we passed in the hall, we'd nod or wave, but that was it.

One Monday morning in the spring, the school was agog about Marla's wild Saturday night at the drive-in movies with some older boys. As we neared each other in the hall between classes, she slowed down, gave a pitiful smile and, face flushed, said hi to me.

And I cut her dead, just like all the other Nice Girls did that day. Decades later, I haven't forgotten the look on her face as I turned away from her.

Marla ended up dropping out of school. I was told she later went to prison on drug charges. She's now living 150 miles from our hometown but didn't come to our latest milestone high school reunion.

I'm under no illusions that a smile or "hi" on that day would have changed Marla's life trajectory the way Jesus' "Follow me" changed Matthew's. But I've been immensely blessed that on the days of my worst sins, people didn't shun me, nor did the Lord. And as I sit here, looking at Marla's Facebook page, I'm thinking about sending a friend request: not to assuage my conscience but to relive those memories of the summer after eighth grade.

PONDERING OUTSIDERS

- Read Matthew 9:9 aloud. Jesus' words are simple: "Follow me." Matthew responds not with words but with action: he gets up and follows. What is Jesus asking of you today, and how can you just do it rather than making excuses or promises for the future?
- You avoid a family member or friend because every encounter results in an argument. Maybe avoiding that person is the right thing for now. If so, consider praying that the Lord might soften your hearts and tongues in the future.
- Maybe you have been the outsider so long in your family, your parish, or your job that you relish the role. Do a spiritual checkup: Have you also become deaf to Jesus' call to follow, not just to go to Mass and receive the sacraments but to live a Christlike life?

MATTHEW IN IMAGES

The Italian painter Caravaggio (1571–1610) brought ambiguity into his *The Calling of Saint Matthew*.[39] The light coming through a window highlights Jesus' hand and the faces of some of the men at the table. It is unclear whether the man with the beard is pointing at himself, the man whose head is in his hands, or the person to the bearded man's right.

Think about a time when your response to Jesus' call has been "Who, me?" or "Do you mean him?" Why are you avoiding Jesus' request?

The French painter James Tissot (1836–1902) spent the first part of his career painting the people of high society. A vision around the time of his fiftieth birthday brought him back to an active Catholic faith, and he spent much of the rest of his career painting biblical scenes. In *The Calling of Saint Matthew*,[40] our eyes are immediately drawn to Jesus, clad in white. He places two fingers on Matthew in the tax collection booth. Matthew's face is turned toward Jesus, almost as if Jesus is physically drawing him in. A man, possibly there to pay his taxes, looks on, hand to face, in the upper right corner.

Jesus told Matthew to follow him, but he didn't bring him along by force. In this painting, all it takes for Matthew to leave his old life behind are the words and a light touch. How is Jesus gently asking you to walk more closely with him?

PRAYER

St. Matthew, like you, I know that feeling of being an outsider. Something is missing from my life, and it isn't money or prestige or family or friends. I feel myself moving further and further from Jesus, and I'm not sure why. Please ask the Lord to call me to a deeper relationship as he called you to follow. Amen.

Another Outsider

ST. CHARLES DE FOUCALD

(1858–1916)

CANONIZED MAY 15, 2022 FEAST DAY: MAY 15

Charles's life sounds like something out of an action-adventure movie until you get to the end: born into the French aristocracy, followed by a dissipated youth away from his Catholic faith, then years as a soldier stationed in the Middle East and Africa, followed by...entry into religious life?

Twenty-eight-year-old Charles was back in Paris, preparing for his next adventure, when he found himself among a group of people "who were highly intelligent, highly virtuous, and highly Christian.... Even though I wasn't a believer I started going to church. It was the only place where I felt at ease, and I would spend long hours there repeating this strange prayer: 'My God, if you exist, allow me know you!' But I did not know you...."[41]

Charles returned to his family and faith. His confessor made him wait three years before committing to religious life. He became a Trappist monk, living first in France and later in Turkey. After seven years, he left to serve at a convent near Nazareth. He was ordained a few years later, and then became a hermit in 1890 in the central Sahara. His work, in addition to prayer, included creating a dictionary and grammar for the language of the area's people and translating the gospels for them. The obvious differences in physique and life experiences were bridged by these efforts.

He had been in the desert for nearly thirty years when bandits attacked him, intending to kidnap him for ransom. However, confusion ensued and Charles was shot in the head and died instantly.

Charles appeared to embrace the role of outsider as an opportunity to evangelize. He wrote while in the desert, "My apostolate must be the apostolate of goodness. If someone were to ask why I am gentle and good, I must say, 'because I am the servant of someone who is far better than me.'"[42]

A DEEPER DIVE

...Matthew responds instantly to Jesus' call: "he rose and followed him." The brevity of the sentence clearly highlights Matthew's readiness in responding to the call. For him it meant leaving everything, especially what guaranteed him a reliable source of income, even if it was often unfair and dishonorable. Evidently, Matthew understood that familiarity with Jesus did not permit him to pursue activities of which God disapproved.

■ **POPE BENEDICT XVI**, *General Audience, August 30, 2006*[43]

James Son of Alphaeus

THE ACTION-ORIENTED ONE

DEATH: Around 62 AD in Judaea or modern-day Egypt

FEAST DAY: May 3 (with Philip)

SCRIPTURE: What good is it, my brothers and sisters, if someone claims to have faith but does not have works? Surely that faith cannot save, can it? ■ **JAMES 2:14**

Who Was James Son of Alphaeus?

James appears only in the synoptic gospels (Matthew 10:3; Mark 3:18; Luke 6:15), always as the son of Alphaeus. He does not appear at all in John's gospel. He is also listed with the others in Acts 1:13 at the coming of the Holy Spirit.

Beyond that, things are uncertain.

James is sometimes called James the Less. It is believed this referred to his joining the ministry after James son of Zebedee and brother of John or that this James was younger or shorter.

The *New American Bible* introduction to the Letter of James states that the author of the letter "can scarcely be one of the two members of the Twelve who bore the name James" because the person is called "slave of God and of the Lord Jesus Christ,"[44] not an apostle. The NAB says the writer is most likely James, a relative of Jesus who led the Jewish Christian community in Jerusalem.

However, Pope Benedict, in a general audience on June 28, 2006, said James son of Alphaeus likely was a relative of Jesus (though not a blood brother); the pope also noted that James may have been the son of Mary the wife of Clopas who was at the foot of the cross with the Blessed Virgin and Mary Magdalene in John's gospel.[45] (Some believe Clopas may be a Greek translation of the Aramaic name Alphaeus and that this Mary may have been the Blessed Virgin's sister, half-sister, or sister-in-law.)

The pope talked about James's prominence in the Church at Jerusalem and credited him with the Letter of James. Benedict described the letter as "quite an important writing which heavily insists on the need not to reduce our faith to a purely verbal or abstract declaration, but to express it in practice in good works."[46]

This chapter adopts the pope's viewpoint of James for study purposes.

James may have been crucified in Egypt or stoned to death in Jerusalem. Some believe he was beaten to death with a fuller's club, which is used in wool production to cleanse the cloth. Images often show James carrying such a club to symbolize his martyrdom.

While James and Philip share a feast day, there is no indication they ministered together or were related. Both of their relics reside in Rome at the Basilica of the Holy Apostles, also known as Santi Apostoli.

Old Testament Scripture on **Works**

DEUTERONOMY 15:7

Moses instructs the Israelites on generosity, saying, "do not be hard-hearted or tight-fisted toward your needy neighbor."

PROVERBS 19:17

Solomon reminds the people that "whoever is kind to the poor lends to the Lord, and will be repaid in full."

PSALM 41:1

In his plea for healing and the assurance of God's help, David says, "Happy are those who consider the poor; the Lord delivers them in the day of trouble."

JAMES THE MAN

Maybe James was a late bloomer. Or maybe the likes of the sons of Zebedee and Jonah and their quick wits and bold actions and pronouncements just overwhelmed him.

He and Simon the Zealot/Cananaean are the only ones of the Twelve who do not get at least a passing reference in John's gospel. I'm not sure that would have bothered James. I see him more as a man who watched and thoughtfully considered Jesus' teachings and challenges. He didn't see a need to challenge the way Peter could because he was still processing things. He wasn't focused on his position in the kingdom to come because he was still thinking about how to follow Jesus in the here and now.

Like Jesus and so many of our saints, James knew when his time had come and when his voice needed to be raised. Pope Benedict XVI described James as swinging into action after Pentecost, becoming the leader of the Jewish Christian community. It's possible his ministry took place within ninety miles of Nazareth, where he grew up. But James's letter and its words about the relationship between faith and works continue to challenge all Christians nearly two thousand years later. They are clear and strong. There's no rabbinical parrying, question for question, or talk of shades of gray or exceptions or exemptions. Faith and works, to James, were inseparable.

What if other scholars are right and the son of Alphaeus was not the James credited with the New Testament letter? We do know this: He was called by Jesus for a purpose—a quiet, serene purpose. James appears to have been satisfied without questioning his teacher, with drinking in the lessons, with being so obedient that there are no stories of struggle. Like most of us, he didn't seek the spotlight or stand out in the crowd. His example of deliberate, peaceful surrender is something from which we can all learn.

BEING JAMES TODAY

I heard about Betty for a few years before I met her. Her name was always in the parish bulletin about something or other: the worker-bee tasks like organizing food for a festival or putting together Thanksgiving dinner baskets for people who needed help.

Then came the days when I started having annual paperwork to do with the local government entity because I have a home-based business. Betty's name was on related government websites. Even though her last name is distinctive, I didn't think the church lady and the government leader could possibly be the same person.

Then, finally, I was on a team for a retreat, and Betty signed up. It turned out the same person sponsored us but always figured we knew each other. The retreat was about an hour old before introductions started and a soft-spoken woman about ten years younger than me introduced herself as Betty. She was pretty and well dressed, and throughout the retreat she listened more than she talked.

As we got to know each other, I learned that her education at a Benedictine college thoroughly informs her being: Prayer. Deep listening. And, of course, service, so often linked to hospitality. I also found out she was doing ministry in ways I hadn't even noticed, being the years-long backbone of our diocese's biggest charity ball, quietly offering to babysit for friends in crisis, driving friends to medical appointments, all without seeking earthly praise.

Betty's own life has been upended by health and professional issues in the past year. But despite that, if God measured us all by the same yardstick, I am sure she'd be way ahead of me. She shares information but doesn't complain. She participates in daily Mass as often as she can and continues helping others as much as she can.

Like James, her story may not be known to the world. But the way she conducts her balance of faith and works humbles and inspires people like me, people who are happy to give money to a cause but are loath to commit to getting our hands dirty. Betty is in harmony with God's plan for her, just as it appears James was.

PONDERING WORKS

- Read aloud James 2:26, James's bold statement that faith without works is dead, just as the body without the spirit is dead. Do you believe that? Think about faith and works in your life. Do they feed each other, or are you more comfortable practicing one rather than the other? How might you bring them into harmony?
- Some believe that James was beaten to death by a fuller's club, an instrument used to remove dirt and other contaminants in wool production. Fullers are mentioned elsewhere in Scripture, including in the *New American Bible* account of the Transfiguration ("and his clothes became dazzling white, such as no fuller on earth could bleach them," says Mark 9:3). Unlike sheep, we can always turn away from the Good Shepherd's efforts to cleanse us. Consider putting an image of a fuller's club or a sheepskin as your mobile phone's home screen this week to remind you to be present to the changes the Lord desires in your life.
- For some of us, it's a lot easier to donate money to a cause than it is to donate time, even though we know both are important. Identify a ministry where you can commit to helping one hour a month. Maybe it's stocking shelves at a food pantry or checking in people at a nearby retreat center. Do it a couple of times, then journal about how you felt before, during, and after that service.

JAMES IN IMAGES

James is shown fully alive and calling out in prayer in *Saint James the Less*[47] by French painter James Tissot (1836–1902), part of "The Life of Our Lord Jesus Christ" collection. James, in white garments and with outstretched hands, is the focal point; other than a few trees in the upper right corner, the rest of the work is in shades of gray and beige.

How do you feel about this intimate image of this apostle speaking to God rather than doing good works? Are there places where you can pull out of life's busyness and get away to find God, physically or mentally?

An earlier painter, Italian Nicolò Bambini (1651–1736), showed the risen Christ providing bread to James, whose arms are outstretched in *Christ Appears to St. James the Less*.[48] James, whom we see from behind, is in darkness except for his face; Jesus is depicted in shades of white. Think about a situation in your life where you feel starved in some way. What is Christ offering to satisfy your hunger?

PRAYER

St. James, the world tells me my life has no meaning. Lots of people are better spouses, parents, grandparents, siblings, employees, and friends than I am. Help me to remember that doing love and service in quiet ways is pleasing to the Lord. Amen.

Another Person of Works

ST. MARÍA GUADALUPE GARCÍA ZAVALA

(1878–1963)

CANONIZED MAY 12, 2013 ⁂ FEAST DAY: JUNE 24

Mexico-born María, then known as Anastasia, was twenty-three when it happened. Marriage had always been her desire, and now she was engaged. But Jesus had other plans: he called her to religious life in a public way, helping the underserved.

When she told her spiritual director of this development, he invited her to join him in founding a community to support people who were hospitalized. The young woman took the name Maria in religious life and was named the congregation's superior general. The sisters' works were unending: begging to get money for the hospital; providing quality nursing care regardless of the patients' backgrounds or means; praying on their knees on the hospital floor with patients.

During turbulent times in Mexico, Maria hid the archbishop of Guadalajara and other priests at the hospital, even as she provided care and food to those who lived nearby and were among the Church's persecutors.

In 2013, the woman they called Mother Lupita became Mexico's second female saint. Today, her community continues to do good works in Mexico, Peru, Iceland, Greece, and Italy.

A DEEPER DIVE

Lastly, the Letter of James urges us to abandon ourselves in the hands of God in all that we do: 'If the Lord wills' (James 4:15). Thus, he teaches us not to presume to plan our lives autonomously and with self-interest, but to make room for the inscrutable will of God, who knows what is truly good for us. In this way, St. James remains an ever up-to-date teacher of life for each one of us.

■ **POPE BENEDICT XVI,** *General Audience, June 28, 2006*[49]

Jude Thaddaeus

THE ORDINARY ONE

DEATH: Traditionally, around 66 AD

FEAST DAY: October 28 (with Simon the Zealot / Cananaean)

SCRIPTURE: "Lord, how is it that you will reveal yourself to us, and not to the world?" ▪ **JOHN 14:22**

Who Was Jude Thaddaeus?

The *Catholic Encyclopedia* says the apostle was a Jew raised in Upper Mesopotamia who "came to Jerusalem to worship in the days of John the Baptist; and having heard his preaching and seen his angelic life, he was baptized, and his name was called Thaddaeus."[50]

The apostle is identified as Thaddaeus in two of the synoptic gospels (Mark 3:18 and Matthew 10:3, which includes the footnote "Other ancient authorities read *Lebbaeus*, or *Lebbaeus called Thaddaeus*"). Luke 6:16 refers to "Judas son of James." The listing of those in Acts 1:13 at the coming of the Holy Spirit includes "Judas son of James," with the footnote "or *the brother of*."

Since the other eleven are easily cross-referenced in the synoptic gospels, it is generally accepted that Thaddaeus and Judas the son or brother of James were the same person. Sorting out which James and which Jude is more difficult. Some ancient writers identify Jude Thaddaeus and James the Less as sons of Mary the wife of Clopas, and some believe she was the Blessed Virgin's sister-in-law (Clopas being Joseph's brother). The *Golden Legend*, Jacobus de Voragine's thirteenth-century collection of saints' lives, also identifies Simon the Zealot or Cananaean as a brother of Jude Thaddaeus and James the Less. Since James the Great and John are consistently identified as "the sons of Zebedee," it seems a bit curious that if James the Less, Simon the Zealot or Cananaean, and Jude Thaddaeus were brothers, the writers did not chronicle that.

John's gospel mentions "Judas (not Iscariot)" once, at the Last Supper. The apostle's question comes after the washing of the apostles' feet, after Thomas and Philip's comments, and immediately after Jesus promises the coming of the Holy Spirit. "Lord, how is it that you will reveal yourself to us and not to the world?" (John 14:22). Jesus doesn't answer him directly; he talks about love and the Father and keeping Jesus' words, and says the Holy Spirit "will teach you everything and remind you of all that I have said to you" (John 14:26).

We don't know where Jude Thaddaeus or most of the apostles were as Jesus was crucified; they may have been among the acquaintances Luke 23:49 says were standing at a distance.

The *New American Bible* introduction to the Letter of Jude[51] notes that the author is not referred to as an apostle and is "almost certainly" the Jude who appears among Jesus' relatives in Matthew 13:55 and Mark 6:3. A James also appears in those two verses. However, in a 2006 general audience, Pope Benedict XVI directly linked Jude Thaddaeus to the letter.[52]

Old Testament Scripture on **Ordinariness**

1 SAMUEL 16:7

When Samuel looks upon Eliab and believes he must be the anointed one, the Lord's response is that the Almighty looks on the heart, not the outward appearance.

JUDGES 6:15–16

Gideon protests that he is too weak to deliver Israel; the Lord promises to be with him and foresees victory.

JEREMIAH 1:8

When Jeremiah says he is too young to be a prophet to the nations, the Lord promises the boy, "I am with you to deliver you."

This chapter adopts the pope's viewpoint of Jude Thaddaeus for study purposes.

What the apostle did after Pentecost in general is murky. In some legends, a pagan mob killed him in Beirut, Lebanon. Others say he and Simon the Zealot or Cananaean preached together in what is now Iran, and Jude Thaddaeus then was martyred with an ax.

The Armenian Apostolic Church, which has not been in communion with the Roman Catholic Church since 451, believes Jude Thaddaeus was martyred in Armenia, and that St. Thaddeus Monastery, or Qara Kelisa, now in northwest Iran, was built on his grave. The monastery is now on the United Nations Educational, Scientific, and Cultural Organization (UNESCO) World Heritage and Intangible Cultural Heritage lists.[53] Pilgrims from the Armenian Apostolic Church travel more than four hundred miles to visit the site on the apostle's feast day, the one day it is open for visitors each year.

JUDE THADDEUS THE MAN

Jude Thaddaeus just couldn't grasp it: Why wouldn't Jesus reveal himself to the entire world when he returned? You can almost see the apostle scratching his head: "Why *shouldn't* everyone be embraced by the Messiah? How is he going to do it? What makes us—*me*—worthy?"

After all, Jude Thaddaeus appears to have been a simple man, one of little drama. We see nothing of his call from Jesus or of his evangelism in the gospels. Jesus doesn't draw him in close in the same way he does Peter, James the Great, John, or even Andrew. He is never in a group of apostles whom Jesus brings into less than public signs and wonders, and we never see a smaller group conversation with Jesus where Jude Thaddaeus is present. He had to have known he's not in the inner circle, but we see no indication that bothers him.

He's not like Thomas and Philip at the Last Supper. John 14 tells us Thomas wanted to know the way, and Philip wanted to see the Almighty right then and there. He's not like Peter, who first doesn't want his feet washed by Jesus, then wants his hands and head washed too. Nor is he like Judas the Iscariot, who is biding his time to leave and betray. And he has never jockeyed for position the way the sons of Zebedee do.

Maybe, just maybe, Jude Thaddaeus is like most of us.

His Last Supper question tugs at our hearts and souls in a way that what the others ask doesn't: "Lord, how is it that you will reveal yourself to us, and not to the world?" (John 14:22). Some posit that Jude Thaddaeus was envisioning Jesus returning as some sort of a ghost that only the apostles could see. Others think this apostle, like the others, did not grasp that Jesus was not going to come back and sit on an earthly throne, bedecked with jewels and other trappings.

I'm fond of one of the possibilities expressed by Puritan theologian John Gill (1697–1771): that Jude Thaddaeus's question may have come

> from an honest hearty desire that the glory of Christ might not be confined to a few only; but that the whole world might see it, and be filled with it: or rather from his modesty, and the sense he had of his own unworthiness, and of the rest of the apostles, to have such a peculiar manifestation of Christ to them, when they were no more deserving of it than others: the question is put by him with admiration and astonishment; and as not being able to give, or think of any other reason of such a procedure, but the amazing grace of Christ, his free favor and sovereign will and pleasure.[54]

Because really, isn't that something we all think at times in the depths of our souls, that while we believe, we surely aren't worthy? Of course, we aren't. Grace is free, and so is God's love. When we get out of our own way and believe that and act accordingly, we are that much closer to the possibility of eternal life. That, in essence, was Jesus' response to Jude Thaddeus.

The Letter of Jude dovetails nicely with the view that at the Last Supper, Jude Thaddaeus was trying to figure out "Why us?" It warns the readers of false teachers and emphasizes that "Jesus, who saved a people out of the land of Egypt, afterward destroyed those who did not believe" (Jude 1:5). He encourages them to "build yourselves up on your most holy faith" and pray in the Holy Spirit (Jude 1:20), and to "keep yourselves in the love of God" (Jude 1:21). The letter's closing benediction speaks directly to those who, like Jude Thaddaeus before the coming of the Holy Spirit, wondered, "Why me? I'm not good enough": "Now to him who is able to keep you from falling, and to make you stand without blemish in the presence of his glory with rejoicing, to the only God our Savior, through Jesus Christ our Lord, be glory, majesty, power, and authority, before all time and now and forever. Amen" (Jude 1:24–25).

Small wonder that believers throughout the ages have turned to him for intercession when they feel desperate. He gets us.

BEING JUDE THADDEUS TODAY

In confession a few months after I'd returned to the Church after thirty-three years away, I was concerned about how my efforts to do God's will seemed to be failing big time. I signed up to peel potatoes for a parish event but ended up emceeing part of the festivities on the fly. I signed up for what I thought was helping with doughnuts after the 7:30 a.m. Mass but ended up on the parish council. I signed up for a short-term Bible study to learn more about Jesus and ended up facilitating some of the sessions.

"I don't want to stand out," I told the pastor. "I just want to work in the background, do my good works in secret."

He sighed and ran his fingers through his thinning hair. He shut his eyes for a few seconds, and I began to wonder whether I should have brought this up. But it was what was on my soul. I was twisting about it at 3 a.m.

He opened his eyes. "Look, Melanie. You're what, six feet tall? You're going to stand out. God made you that way. Deal with it."

Strangely, it helped, and I have accepted, with humility I hope, the gifts God gave me and have used them for the Almighty's glory: Proclaiming Scripture. Public speaking. Writing. Facilitating Bible study.

My gifts are no better than yours or Jude Thaddaeus's. They're just different, as Paul says so beautifully in Romans 12:6: "We have gifts that differ according to the grace given to us...."

I'm a people watcher. Some of my holiest moments come as I watch the Jude Thaddaeuses in my world being extraordinary in their ordinariness:

- The high-powered lobbyist who ushered at the 7:30 a.m. Mass for years, softly and gently welcoming people as they came in and finding seats for everyone, including on Easter Sunday.
- The woman who arranges the altar flowers so beautifully, with no credit in the bulletin or on the website.
- The couple who paid an out-of-work friend's rent for more than a year, and no one knew until he told people when he moved out of the area.

- The homeschooling mom of nine who also supports her husband's and eldest daughter's entrepreneurial efforts, helps another daughter's Heritage Girls group, frequently has priests over for a good home-cooked meal, and has the wisdom to find time for personal retreats.

You know people just like them, or maybe you're one of them. Please know that God appreciates your unsung service, just as Jude Thaddaeus was appreciated. Your gifts are more noticeable than you realize.

PONDERING ORDINARINESS

- Read aloud Jude 1:24–25. How can you rely more on Jesus and less on yourself to resist the world's temptations?
- Plenty of people in your parish do the work without fanfare every day. They are the ones who set up snacks for your Bible study group or organize rides to workcamp or see that the sacred linens and vessels are clean. Identify one of these good souls, and thank the person in person or give him or her a card of thanks.
- Maybe public roles come naturally to you. You're good at being a lector, cantoring, leading parish council, and the like. Examine your motivations to make sure your service is about the Lord, not you. Recalibrate as needed.

JUDE THADDEUS IN IMAGES

The Flemish painter Anthony van Dyck's (1599–1641) work *The Apostle Judas Thaddeus* depicts him with wavy auburn hair and beard.[55] His face is slightly lined; other than the black of his cloak, much of the rest of the portrait is in shades of brown. One could see this man in the working class of any generation.

Study the apostle's eyes. What is he looking at? Neither their set nor his hidden mouth give us any clues.

Jude Thaddaeus is older in *Apostle St. Thaddeus (Jude)* by the Spaniard El Greco (1541–1614).[56] The apostle's hair is graying, and he wears a red cloak. His eyes look directly at us, almost challenging us.

Consider what the painter might have been attempting to show with the apostle's piercing eyes. Perhaps it's a reminder to consider what the Lord sees when he looks into your soul. How can you make it more appealing to him?

PRAYER

St. Jude Thaddaeus, I'll never be pope, president, or even a big-time social media influencer. Please help me to see that being myself and surrendering my own fears and will to Jesus is enough, in this world and the next. Amen.

Another Ordinary One

ST. ANDRÉ BESSETTE *(1845–1937)*

CANONIZED OCTOBER 17, 2010 ❧ FEAST DAY: JANUARY 6

It was not an auspicious start to life, and it quickly got worse. André, born Alfred in a small town southeast of Montreal, was so sickly at birth that he received a conditional baptism when he was only a day old. He had four older siblings; four others had died as infants. By the time he was twelve, both his parents had died. He struck out on his own as a factory worker in Quebec and the United States, all but illiterate and still in poor health. To the world, he didn't count for much.

When he was twenty-five, André attempted to enter religious life with the Holy Cross Brothers in Montreal. Despite a letter from his pastor that read, "I am sending you a saint," André was rejected initially. The bishop of Montreal got involved; the young man was accepted and took the name Brother André. Given his health issues and lack of education, he was assigned to be the porter at the brothers' boarding school. He also helped as a janitor, launderer, courier, barber, and sacristan, but porter was the role where he encountered students, teachers, and visitors.

His friendly manner encouraged people to tell him their troubles. He prayed with and for them and encouraged them to pray to St. Joseph, to whom André had had a devotion since childhood. Many experienced healing, and so the stories about him spread, and more and more people came to the door or wrote André letters. He always reminded them that the healing came from St. Joseph, not him, and offered this counsel: "Do not seek to have your trials removed; ask rather for the grace to bear them well."[57]

A DEEPER DIVE

It is easy to see that the author [of the closing verses of the Letter of Jude] lived to the full his own faith, to which realities as great as moral integrity and joy, trust and lastly praise belong, since it is all motivated solely by the goodness of our one God and the mercy of our Lord Jesus Christ.

■ **POPE BENEDICT XVI**, *General Audience, October 11, 2006*[58]

Simon the Zealot or Cananaean

THE ONE WITH ZEAL

DEATH: Mid- to late-1st century AD

FEAST DAY: October 28 (with Jude Thaddaeus)

SCRIPTURE: It is zeal for your house that has consumed me; the insults of those who insult you have fallen on me. ■ **PSALM 69:9**

Who Was Simon?

The apostle is identified as Simon the Cananaean in Mark 3:18 and Matthew 10:4; Luke 6:15 names him "Simon, who was called the Zealot." Acts 1:13 also calls him "Simon the Zealot" in the description of the coming of the Holy Spirit.

Other than those verses, this Simon doesn't appear in the New Testament. He was at the Last Supper with the rest of the Twelve, of course. We don't know where he or most of the apostles were as Jesus was crucified; they may have been among the acquaintances Luke 23:49 says were standing at a distance.

Was Simon a member of the Zealot political group or a Cananaean? It's hard to say. The Zealots were most prominent around the time of the first Jewish-Roman War (66–73 AD). That group gave no quarter to Rome and its polytheism; they were in essence enemies not only of the Romans but also of Jews who sought to get along with the Romans. It is possible Simon was involved with the Zealots before following Jesus; in 6 AD, people who identified as Zealots opposed a Roman-ordered census of Galilee. That likely was around the time Simon was born. But as noted above, the group did not become formally known and organized as the Zealots until a few decades after the Ascension.

While St. Jerome read the reference in ancient writings to *Kananaios* or *Kananites* to mean that Simon was from Cana, later experts believe that that is a mistranslation. More likely, Simon was a Galilean, as were all the Twelve by birth or residence.

The Orthodox Church identifies Simon as the bridegroom at the wedding at Cana, where Jesus turned water into wine. That tradition holds that the event changed Simon's life and made him an impassioned follower of Jesus. This, however, is not part of the Roman Catholic tradition.

Others have attempted to connect this apostle to other Simons: there are at least nine of them in the New Testament, not counting other early Church leaders named Simon who were not mentioned in Scripture. For example, the second bishop of Jerusalem—Simeon of Jerusalem or Simon of Clopas—according to Roman Catholic tradition succeeded in that position the martyred apostle James son of Alphaeus. There is some thought that this bishop could be Simon the Apostle, but that is by no means generally accepted. There's also speculation in non-Catholic circles that Simon the bishop could be the relative of Jesus mentioned in Matthew 13:55 and Mark 6:3.

The *Golden Legend*, Jacobus de Voragine's thirteenth-century collection of saints' lives, also identifies this Simon as a brother of Jude Thaddaeus and James son of Alphaeus. But since James the Great and John are consistently identified as "the sons of Zebedee," and Peter and Andrew are clearly brothers, it seems a bit curious that if this Simon, James son of Alphaeus, and Jude Thaddaeus were brothers, the writers did not chronicle that.

De Voragine says Simon preached in Egypt, and then with Jude Thaddaeus in what is now Iran. According to this source, both were martyred in 65 AD. However, there is a lack of consensus as to where Simon preached or what happened to him. Other traditions put him in Samaria or in Britain, where he was said to have been crucified. Still others say he died peacefully in Turkey. His relics are at the St. Joseph's Altar at St. Peter's Basilica in Rome and elsewhere.

Old Testament Scripture on **Zeal**

PSALM 18:1
After the Lord delivers David from Saul and his other enemies, the king offers a psalm of praise, beginning with "I love you, O Lord, my strength."

SIRACH 51:18
In sharing his story, Ben Sira says, "For I resolved to practice wisdom, and I was zealous for the good, and I shall never be disappointed."

1 MACCABEES 2:27
Upon seeing the blasphemies being committed in Judah and Jerusalem, Matthias becomes violent, then cries out, "Let every one who is zealous for the law and supports the covenant come out with me!"

SIMON THE MAN

Simon didn't leave epistles to guide the early Church and inspire us today. But even a somewhat fanciful account by a writer who never knew Simon makes him sound like someone I'd want in my corner. "This holy man had in him obedience of the commandments by execution, heaviness by pity of torment, and had love of souls by firm ardor of love," de Voragine wrote of Simon.

Those are the type of words dictionaries use even today to define zeal, an energetic or emotional pursuit.

A description by Pope Benedict XVI resonates with me. Even if Simon was not a member of the Zealots movement, "he was at least marked by passionate attachment to his Jewish identity, hence, for God, his People and divine Law," the pope said in a general audience on October 11, 2006.[59] The pope contrasted the differences between Simon and Matthew the tax collector, then noted what they had in common: "...Jesus called his disciples and collaborators, without exception, from the most varied social and religious backgrounds. It was people who interested him, not social classes or labels!"

Those who are zealous for the Lord live and breathe the Word. They're not perfect, but they tend not to reside in their own heads very much, worried about what others are thinking or saying about them. It's not that they don't want to be liked and respected, but they know who they serve and that nothing the world offers can compare to pleasing God.

BEING SIMON TODAY

I've known the Johnsons for twenty years. Most people in our parish would recognize them, though they probably don't know their names.

Why would they recognize a couple in their sixties who don't talk loudly or dress flamboyantly? Because the Johnsons are always there. Always have been, with zeal for God and community. They're both secular Franciscans, and in their quiet, unassuming way they live St. Francis of Assisi's gospel spirit every day.

Ann has taught hundreds of souls how to be good sacristans. For years, when no one else was to be found, she'd be setting up chairs in the gym for overflow Christmas and Easter Masses. She also is the woman who slips a dozen hard-boiled eggs or a homemade casserole on the table at any gathering, never drawing attention to herself by telling everyone how good her recipe is or warning people this is the first time she's ever made it or policing people saying that the dish is supposed to serve ten so don't take too much.

Jim is an extraordinary minister of Holy Communion. And a lector. And an usher. And a part of the choir when not enough members show up, as has been known to happen at the 5 a.m. Advent novena the Filipino community put on for years. Jim's not Filipino and isn't well versed in the Tagalog language, but when a voice is needed, he's there.

They drive people to Mass and back, to medical appointments, and more. There's never a complaint about having to leave their home early or miss part of the fun at a parish event because someone needed a ride and the Johnsons were their transportation.

Their son and daughter, now in their late twenties and married with kids of their own, were both reliable, steady altar servers when they were younger. Newbie EMs and sacristans were known to ask Jane and Andy for advice and help if their parents weren't around.

Ann recently told me that years ago, her daughter asked why the four of them had to do a task of drudgery at our parish and wondered why someone else couldn't do it. Ann and Jim's son replied, "Because we're Johnsons. It's what we do."

Jim and Ann are both retired now, and Ann has a chronic condition that impedes her mobility. So, the two of them and their daughter's family have bought a home about seventy miles away, where Jim and Ann can live on one level and their daughter's family on the other. As soon as the ADA-compliant bathroom is done, they'll be leaving the place they lived for decades. While it's a little scary, you can tell they're already thinking about ways they can serve God and their new community—with zeal.

PONDERING ZEAL

- Read aloud all of Psalm 69. Contemplate David's prayer, first sharing the way he is persecuted, then humbly asking the Lord for help at a time of the Almighty's choosing, and confidently closing with praise. It's akin to the Lord's Prayer model of adoration, confession, thanksgiving, and supplication, though ordered differently. Structure your deepest prayer today as David would have.

- Simon didn't leave behind a body of written work, so it may be safe to assume that his zealousness for God came through his actions. Can you do the same with a loved one who is away from faith? Can you show your love and devotion to God rather than sharing your fears about the loved one missing out on the hope of eternal life?
- Examine the way you do your favorite ministry, whether it's fund raising or organizing the annual Christmas bazaar or serving as an extraordinary minister of the Eucharist. Are there times your zeal is for you and getting attention for a job well done rather than for God?

SIMON IN IMAGES

In *Saint Simon*, Spanish painter Jusepe de Ribera (1591–1652) gives us a mysterious look at the apostle.[60] His face is almost entirely in the dark. We see only his forehead and the area around his left eye. He appears to be carrying a leather bag of some sort, and perhaps a saw, because of the tradition that he was sawed in half.

Why do you think Ribera chose to show us so little of Simon? Perhaps because so little is known about him? Where would you cast light on this painting if you could?

Flemish artist Anthony van Dyck (1599–1641), in *The Apostle Saint Simon*,[61] shows us a young, pensive apostle. His reddish-brown hair is nearly the same color as his clothing. He is clean shaven. His brown eyes seem as though they've seen much as he looks out at us, and the set of his mouth is somber and determined.

Look at your own photos. Is there one that shows your zeal for God, rather than having a good time with family and friends? If not, think about what your "zeal" expression would be.

PRAYER

St. Simon, the world knows little about you beyond your zealousness for God. I ask that you help me understand that that is enough—and that is all. Remind me, please, that it doesn't matter how many social media followers I have or how many birthday or Christmas greetings I receive if my heart and soul are not focused on the Almighty. Amen.

Another One with Zeal

ST. JOSÉ BROCHERO *(1840–1914)*

CANONIZED OCTOBER 16, 2016 FEAST DAY: JANUARY 26

Like Simon, José didn't write beautiful letters to the faithful or give rousing homilies or lectures. He did his ministry among under-served populations in central Argentina's Great Highlands region, wearing a poncho and sombrero and riding a mule. "There'll be trouble if the devil robs me of a single soul!"[62] the tireless priest was known to say.

Just weeks before his own death, Pope Francis spoke of Brochero during an audience with the Community of the Argentine Priests' College in Rome. He shared the saint's zeal for working "for the good of one's neighbor until the last [moment] of one's life."

"As arduous as his task was," Francis said of Brochero, "he tried never to abandon it, even spending most of the night out in the open, in the middle of the cornfields, waiting for them to wake at the farm...so that he could go in to celebrate" the Eucharist.[63]

Brochero showed his zeal by literally bringing people to Christ in his nearly 80-square-mile parish. In addition to offering prayers and sacraments, he helped design and build almost 125 miles of roads along with post offices and telegraph stations, highways, and aqueducts.

The saint contracted Hansen's disease, formerly known as leprosy. He continued to work as a pastor until 1908, then went to live with his sisters for the six years before his death.

A DEEPER DIVE

James, Thaddaeus, Simon the Canaanite, Judas Iscariot. These were good "seconds"; men who could carry out, in all practical detail, what was arranged by the leaders. Not thinkers, and so not doubters; men who wanted something to do, and found themselves satisfied with the doing. Such men are still among us.

■ **R. TUCK,** *Episcopal priest*[64]

Judas Iscariot

THE LOST ONE

DEATH: 30–33 AD in Jerusalem

SCRIPTURE: Jesus said to him, "Friend, do what you are here to do."
■ **MATTHEW 26:50**

Who Was Judas?

Judas is identified as one of the Twelve in each of the synoptic gospels (Mark 3:19; Matthew 10:4; Luke 6:16).

All four gospels delve into Judas's agreement to betray Jesus and the actual betrayal and arrest of Jesus (Matthew 26:14–16, 47–50; Mark 14:10–11, 43–45; Luke 22:3–6, 47–48; John 13:21–30, 18:2–5). Mark provides no reason or rationale for Judas's decision. Matthew indicates money was the driving force. Luke 22:3 as well as John 6:71 and 13:2 state that Judas was a betrayer or that the Satan had entered him.

John 12:4–8 shares Mary of Bethany anointing Jesus' feet with expensive nard and Judas's outrage, saying the real reason Judas cared was that he controlled the common purse and was stealing from it.

The three synoptic gospels offer in essence the same warning from Jesus at the Last Supper: that the betrayer would have been better off not to have been born (Mark 14:21; Luke 22:21–22; Matthew 26:24).

Matthew (27:3–8) describes Judas as remorseful after the betrayal, flinging the thirty pieces of silver at the chief priests and then hanging himself. The chief priests take the money but can't put it in the treasury because it is tainted. They instead buy a plot, known as "the Field of Blood," to bury "foreigners."

No other gospel mentions Judas's death. In Acts 1:18, Luke notes parenthetically that Judas bought a field, fell headlong, and "burst open in the middle and all his bowels gushed out."

The two accounts are not necessarily at odds; the Acts description could align with Matthew's, depending on Judas's decomposition state. Some early extra-biblical writings suggest other followers were responsible for Judas's death; others posit that Judas did not die until later, a swollen, infected caricature of a person.

The spot where Judas is believed to have died by suicide is now home to St. Onuphrius, a Greek Orthodox monastery south of the Old City of Jerusalem. The monastery was built in 1892.

Old Testament Scripture on **Betrayal**

PSALM 55:13–16
David initially calls for the death of a friend who taunts him, then expresses faith that "the Lord will save me."

2 SAMUEL 17:23
Ahithophel, who once was a counselor to David, backs Absalom in the son's effort to usurp David. David sends another ally as a counteragent, and Absalom listens to that advice instead. Ahithophel believes that since his advice was not followed, Absalom will fail and so returns to his hometown and hangs himself.

ISAIAH 31:6
The prophet exhorts the Israelites to return to God, "whom you have deeply betrayed."

JUDAS THE MAN

Judas likely was an outsider from the beginning. Perhaps that's the way he wanted it.

One tradition is that most, if not all, of the other eleven apostles were from Galilee. They may have known or known of each other while they were growing up and beginning their adult lives.

But Judas's surname, Iscariot, likely means he was from southern Judea town of Kerioth-hezron, mentioned by Joshua in the towns belonging to the tribe of Judah (Joshua 15:25). The town was near what is now the Egypt-Israel border. He moved to Galilee at some point; we don't know when.

We see Jesus' "follow me" call to many of the Twelve in the gospels, but not to Judas. There is no indication of how the two met or how Judas was invited to join the ministry. Nor do we see any interactions between him and the other eleven, positive or negative.

From John's gospel, we know Judas held the common purse, so he may have had some background in finance. Or, he may not have; to our twenty-first-century eyes, Matthew the tax collector seems the logical person to keep track of income and expenses, but our eyes are not Jesus'. Being the finance guy likely would have meant some conversations with Jesus and others about their funds, but we don't see that. That's not a surprise; the gospels' purpose is to share Jesus' ministry and sacrifice, not the human dynamics among his followers.

But we wonder about Judas—and ourselves.

Not long after the feeding of the five thousand, many disciples left Jesus when he taught about the True Presence at a synagogue in Capernaum. They were repulsed by what they thought he was saying: that human flesh and blood would be eaten. All of the Twelve, including Judas, stayed, with Peter perhaps speaking for all: "Lord, to whom can we go? You have the words of eternal life" (John 6:68). But just seconds later, Jesus' response includes the information that one of the Twelve is a devil. John 6:71 tells us it is Judas.

Luke's and John's references to a devil being in Judas trouble us today, as do Jesus' own statements that it would have better for his betrayer not to have been born. Was Judas truly predestined to be despised for all time as a traitor, a defector of who and what he had professed to believe for three years? What if he had asked Jesus for help in repelling the demon? Does his repentance (Matthew 27:3–10) count for nothing? Like the early followers, we live in a fallen world and sometimes make bad choices—really, really bad choices,

choices that can cause great physical, mental, and emotional harm to others and to ourselves and grieve the Almighty. What about this *Catechism of the Catholic Church* teaching?

> There is no offense, however serious, that the Church cannot forgive. "There is no one, however wicked and guilty, who may not confidently hope for forgiveness, provided his repentance is honest." ▪ *CCC 982*

For centuries, minds far more gifted than mine have debated Judas's motivation and potential salvation. There's a school of thought that Judas in essence signed his own eternal damnation warrant by not seeking pardon for his sin. As you can tell, this is something I can get twisted in knots about. (Yes, scrupulosity is one of my greatest temptations.) But I find comfort in one thing: belief in God's grace and mercy.

Throughout the gospels, Jesus rarely calls people "friend" when he's talking with them directly. He uses the word when he is talking about Lazarus to the disciples and in parables; to the paralytic he heals (Luke 5:20); and to someone who calls out to him in a crowd (Luke 12:14). In John 15:13–15, he tells the apostles they are his friends if they do what he commands and that they are no longer his servants because he has made everything known to them.

But the last time he uses the term during his life on earth is after Judas arrives with the armed crowd. After Judas kisses him to identify him to the authorities, Jesus says to him, "Friend, do what you are here to do" (Matthew 26:50).

Would Jesus really have called this despicable man his friend if all hope was lost for Judas? I don't think so.

BEING JUDAS TODAY

When I returned to full communion with the Church, I loved the Sacrament of Penance and Reconciliation. Maybe it was because I had so many capital sins on my soul, and it took a few stumbles and falls before some of them were gone. Unlike when I was a kid and went in the confessional box shaking, I appreciated being able to talk with a priest face to face, knowing that in that moment, I was no longer talking to my pastor or a visiting priest, but through him to God.

I went to confession monthly for several years and looked forward to that "be made clean" feeling as I exited and prayed or did my penance.

Then, well, things got busy, and confession got crowded out. I'd go once a quarter or so in my parish confessional, then at two or three conferences each year. I told myself I didn't need the sacrament as often because I'd conquered a lot of demons. Looking back, that's when that sin of pride started worming its way deeper into me.

Covid came, and there wasn't an opportunity for the sacrament anywhere near me for months. When things began to return to normal, I decided twice a year at conferences would be fine. (That sin of pride again.) I had seen a priest in my parish come out of the confessional almost roaring at a woman because he didn't think her son was adequately prepared to be in the box. I decided I was never going to him again. (Pride again, right? And of course priests have bad days, something this one probably confessed the next time he received the sacrament.)

Holy Week 2025 rolled around. I hadn't been to any Catholic conferences or confession in an entire year, I realized. Me, who professes to love the sacrament's healing power.

As I did my examen, I boiled my sins down to two causes: 1. Too much handwringing about the state of the world and my inability to do anything about it other than be anxious and eat and drink too much. 2. Not going to confession, because saying those things out loud instead of letting them fester, especially at 3 a.m., would have taken away the foothold evil was making in my life.

As God would have it, the priest hearing confessions that day was the one who had yelled at the mother more than a year earlier, the one I swore I would never go to again.

The outcome? He listened. Provided some helpful counsel. Gave me one Our Father and one Hail Mary for my penance. I suspect he discerned I had already beaten myself up mentally and spiritually more than God desired.

As I write this, I wonder what would have happened if Judas had gone to Jesus at any point and said, "Look, I'm in way over my head here. I don't like what I'm becoming, and I'm sorry for what I've done. Please help me be better."

PONDERING THE LOST

- Read the full *Catechism* paragraph 982 on forgiveness aloud.[65] Is there an offense for which you have repented and have been absolved but continue to believe is unforgiveable? Consider scheduling a counseling session with a priest or trained therapist.
- Isolation and unworthiness are two of the devil's favorite lies. That person who always comes to Mass alone and sits in front of you may be struggling. Next week, introduce yourself after the benediction. Think about asking the person to join you for coffee. That could make the devil really angry—yay!

- When in the past have you been the outsider? The only one in your extended family or your group of friends who didn't go to college, didn't get married, didn't have children, didn't have grandchildren? Or maybe it was when you started a new job or moved to a new city. Write down three things you learned from that experience and tuck them away for the next time you feel like "the only one."

JUDAS IN IMAGES

He looks alone and defeated. Brazilian painter José Ferraz de Almeida Júnior (1850–99), in *Judas's Remorse*, shows Judas in red clothing, cloak in his lap, thirty pieces of silver by his side.[66] Three crucifixes and a crowd appear in the distance behind him to the right. Judas's face is almost totally obscured by his beard, some sort of head covering, and shadows.

Remember a time when you felt isolated from the world due to your own actions. Journal about how your faith, however weak at that moment, sustained you and kept you from descending into total despair as Judas did.

Judas Iscariot[67] by English painter William Etty (1787–1849) depicts Judas as an everyman. The work is in essence a bust, showing the apostle in a blue-green tunic against a yellow and red background, with a pillar of brown, possibly representing Jesus' crucifix, possibly the tree from which Judas hanged himself. Judas's head is turned slightly; his face looks strong, his eyes penetrating.

What moment do you think the artist is showing? Judas before the devil came into him? When he was listening to Jesus tell him to do quickly what he had to do? Are there any similarities to photos of you when you were having a spiritual or mental challenge?

PRAYER

Jesus, while I did not betray your earthly life, there are times when my rejection of what you desire of me has grieved us both. Please hold my hand so that I may remember forgiveness is always available when I come to you with a contrite spirit and a desire to sin no more. Amen.

Another Lost One
BROTHER ALESSANDRO SERENELLI *(1882–1970)*

Alessandro was not a saint. In fact, he killed one. But her spoken trust that he could be forgiven and saved is a beautiful story of redemption and conversion.

You likely know the basic facts: Maria Goretti (1890–1902) was just eleven years old when Alessandro and his father shared a farmhouse south of Rome with Maria and her mother and siblings. Alessandro entered the Goretti home, intending to rape Maria. She fought him off, but only after he had stabbed her repeatedly. The next day, suffering from her mortal wounds, she identified Alessandro to authorities and said she forgave him and wanted to see him in heaven.

Alessandro was taken into custody almost immediately. Since he was still a minor, his sentence was thirty years in prison rather than life. After three years, he told a local bishop that Maria had come to him in a dream and given him lilies. He became a model prisoner and ultimately was released in 1929.

Five years later, he visited Maria's mother, begging forgiveness. She had much cause to turn him away; in addition to losing Maria, the crime had resulted in the impoverished Goretti family being split up. But the mother said she could not refuse since Maria had already forgiven him.

Alessandro eventually ended up at a Capuchin monastery, where he worked as a gardener and doorman. Later, the Capuchins accepted him as a religious brother.

Maria was canonized on June 24, 1950. Her mother and four siblings were there. And so, we are told, was Alessandro.

A DEEPER DIVE

One thing that draws my attention is that Jesus never called him a "traitor"; he says that he will be betrayed, but he never called him a "traitor." He never said: "Go away, traitor!" Never! Rather, He calls him "friend," and kisses him....How did Judas end up? I am not sure. Jesus makes a strong threat, here; he makes a strong threat: "Woe to that man by whom the Son of Man is betrayed. It would be better for that man if he had never been born" (see Mt 26:24). But does this mean that Judas is in hell? I do not know. I look at the chapiter. And I hear Jesus' word: "friend."

■ **POPE FRANCIS**, *Homily, April 8, 2020*[68]

ENDNOTES

1 https://www.metmuseum.org/art/collection/search/441971

2 https://commons.wikimedia.org/wiki/File:Pope-peter_pprubens.jpg

3 https://www.vatican.va/content/benedict-xvi/en/audiences/2006/documents/hf_ben-xvi_aud_20060524.html

4 https://www.bible-researcher.com/muratorian.html

5 https://www.agiosandreas.gr/new-cathedral

6 https://commons.wikimedia.org/wiki/Category:The_Calling_of_Saints_Peter_and_Andrew_by_Caravaggio#/media/File:Michelangelo_Merisi_da_Caravaggio_(Milan_1571-Port'_Ercole_1610)_-_The_Calling_of_Saints_Peter_and_Andrew_-_RCIN_402824_-_Hampton_Court_Palace.jpg

7 https://commons.wikimedia.org/wiki/File:Artus_Wolffort_-_St_Andrew_-_WGA25857.jpg

8 https://www.carloacutis.com/en/association/carlo-e-il-suo-kit-per-diventare-santi

9 https://www.miracolieucaristici.org

10 https://www.vatican.va/content/benedict-xvi/en/audiences/2006/documents/hf_ben-xvi_aud_20060614.html

11 https://portal.sds.ox.ac.uk/articles/online_resource/E00172_Eusebius_of_Caesarea_recounts_the_martyrdom_of_James_the_Apostle_son_of_Zebedee_S00108_combining_information_from_the_Acts_of_the_Apostles_and_the_Hypotyposes_of_Clement_of_Alexandria_late_2nd_c_Account_in_his_Ecclesiastical_History_/13795874

12 https://sammlung.staedelmuseum.de/en/work/saint-james-the-greater

13 https://www.museodelprado.es/coleccion/obra-de-arte/el-apostol-santiago/c2c3450b-6c74-4193-9c46-d2fa625c825c?searchid=40d92706-9645-c759-5edd-bd6ac8b99cc8

14 https://www.vatican.va/content/francesco/en/speeches/2023/may/documents/20230511-patriarca-tawadrosii.html

15 https://biblehub.com/commentaries/mark/10-35.htm

16 https://bible.usccb.org/bible/john/0

17 https://bible.usccb.org/bible/revelation/0

18 https://bible.usccb.org/bible/1john/0

19 https://commons.wikimedia.org/wiki/File:Simone_Cantarini_-_S%C3%A3o_Jo%C3%A3o_Batista_em_Medita%C3%A7%C3%A3o.jpg

20 https://commons.wikimedia.org/w/index.php?search=Alonso+Cano's+%281601–1667%29+Saint+John+and+the+Poisoned+Cup&title=Special%3AMediaSearch&type=image

21 https://www.vatican.va/news_services/liturgy/saints/ns_lit_doc_20000409_beat-Hesselblat_en.html

22 https://www.vatican.va/content/benedict-xvi/en/audiences/2006/documents/hf_ben-xvi_aud_20060705.html

23 https://stphiliptheapostleparish.org/relic-of-st-philip-the-apostle/

24 https://commons.wikimedia.org/wiki/File:Philip_the_Apostle._Detail_of_the_mosaic_in_the_Basilica_of_San_Vitale._Ravena,_Italy.jpg

25 https://www.museodelprado.es/en/the-collection/art-work/saint-philip/a0e78920-8f28-47f5-8cd5-f50ba1dfa8c5?searchid=02191537-36ad-5ddb-0e98-a9ec40a68a22

26 https://www.vatican.va/content/benedict-xvi/en/audiences/2006/documents/hf_ben-xvi_aud_20060906.html

27 https://www.biblestudytools.com/commentaries/gills-exposition-of-the-bible/john-1-46.html

28 https://commons.wikimedia.org/wiki/File:Philip_und_Nathanael.jpg

29 https://commons.wikimedia.org/wiki/File:Rubens_apostel_bartolomeus_grt.jpg

30 https://www.vatican.va/content/benedict-xvi/en/audiences/2006/documents/hf_ben-xvi_aud_20061004.html

31 https://www.santhomechurch.org/our-museum.html

32 https://catholicsindia.in/statistics/

33 https://commons.wikimedia.org/wiki/File:The_Incredulity_of_Saint_Thomas-Caravaggio_(1601-2).jpg

34 https://commons.wikimedia.org/wiki/File:Peter_Paul_Rubens_-_Martyrdom_of_St_Thomas.jpg

35 https://www.chfsisters.com/about/about

36 https://www.vatican.va/content/francesco/en/speeches/2024/may/documents/20240513-chiesa-siro-malabarese.html

37 https://www.newadvent.org/cathen/10056b.htm

38 https://bible.usccb.org/bible/matthew/0

39 https://commons.wikimedia.org/wiki/Category:The_Calling_of_Saint_Matthew_by_Caravaggio#/media/File:Caravaggio_%E2%80%94_The_Calling_of_Saint_Matthew.jpg

40 https://www.brooklynmuseum.org/objects/4485

41 https://www.charlesdefoucauld.org/en/biographie.php

42 https://www.charlesdefoucauld.org/en/biographie.php

43 https://www.vatican.va/content/benedict-xvi/en/audiences/2006/documents/hf_ben-xvi_aud_20060830.html

44 https://bible.usccb.org/bible/james/0

45 https://www.vatican.va/content/benedict-xvi/en/audiences/2006/documents/hf_ben-xvi_aud_20060628.html

46 https://www.vatican.va/content/benedict-xvi/en/audiences/2006/documents/hf_ben-xvi_aud_20060628.html

47 https://www.brooklynmuseum.org/objects/4557

48 https://www.christianiconography.info/Venice%202023/San%20Stae/jamesLessBambini.smal.jpg

49 https://www.vatican.va/content/benedict-xvi/en/audiences/2006/documents/hf_ben-xvi_aud_20060628.html

50 https://www.newadvent.org/fathers/0826.htm

51 https://bible.usccb.org/bible/jude/0

52 https://www.vatican.va/content/benedict-xvi/en/audiences/2006/documents/hf_ben-xvi_aud_20061011.html

53 https://ich.unesco.org/en/RL/pilgrimage-to-the-st-thaddeus-apostle-monastery-01571

54 https://biblehub.com/commentaries/john/14-22.htm

55 https://commons.wikimedia.org/wiki/File:Anthonis_van_Dyck,_Kunsthistorisches_Museum_Wien,_Gem%C3%A4ldegalerie_-_Apostel_Judas_Thadd%C3%A4us_-_GG_6809_-_Kunsthistorisches_Museum.jpg

56 https://commons.wikimedia.org/wiki/File:El_Greco_-_St._Jude_Thaddeus_-_Google_Art_Project.jpg

57 https://www.vatican.va/content/benedict-xvi/en/homilies/2010/documents/hf_ben-xvi_hom_20101017_canonizations.html

58 https://www.vatican.va/content/benedict-xvi/en/audiences/2006/documents/hf_ben-xvi_aud_20061011.html

59 https://www.vatican.va/content/benedict-xvi/en/audiences/2006/documents/hf_ben-xvi_aud_20061011.html

60 https://commons.wikimedia.org/wiki/File:Ribera-san_simon.jpg

61 https://commons.wikimedia.org/wiki/File:Van_Dyck_-_Der_Apostel_Simon,_Um_1618-20.jpg

62 https://www.vatican.va/content/francesco/en/letters/2013/documents/papa-francesco_20130914_beatificazione-brochero.html

63 https://press.vatican.va/content/salastampa/en/bollettino/pubblico/2025/01/16/250116d.html

64 https://biblehub.com/sermons/auth/tuck/representative_christian_characters.htm

65 https://usccb.cld.bz/Catechism-of-the-Catholic-Church/276/

66 https://en.wikipedia.org/wiki/File:Almeida_J%C3%BAnior_-_Remorso_de_Judas,_1880.jpg#/media/File:Almeida_J%C3%BAnior_-_Remorso_de_Judas,_1880.jpg

67 https://commons.wikimedia.org/wiki/File:William_Etty_(1787-1849)_-_Judas_Iscariot_-_VIS.257_-_Sheffield_Galleries_and_Museums_Trust.jpg#/media/File:William_Etty_(1787-1849)_-_Judas_Iscariot_-_VIS.257_-_Sheffield_Galleries_and_Museums_Trust.jpg

68 https://www.vatican.va/content/francesco/en/cotidie/2020/documents/papa-francesco-cotidie_20200408_tra-lealta-e-interesse.html